T0065519

CHOOSE

LIFE TO THE FULLEST

100 DAYS TO CREATE A HABIT OF
THINKING AND LIVING GREAT

SPECIAL EDITION - PART 4

MICAH OWINGS & BECCA GUNYON, MCC

WESTBOW
PRESS®
A DIVISION OF THOMAS NELSON
& ZONDERVAN

WestBow Press books may be ordered through booksellers or by contacting:

WestBow Press
A Division of Thomas Nelson & Zondervan
1663 Liberty Drive
Bloomington, IN 47403
www.westbowpress.com
844-714-3454

ISBN: 978-1-6642-3366-9 (sc)
ISBN: 978-1-6642-3367-6 (e)

Print information available on the last page.

WestBow Press rev. date: 05/20/2021

**Dedicated to our family the Owings,
Gunyons, and Tuiasosopos**

*Written for those who want to develop a
daily routine and habit of thinking great
and inviting Jesus in, which leads to feeling
great, and results in life to the Fullest!*

ENDORSEMENTS

"It's been said that we do not rise to the level of our hopes but rather we fall to the level of our habits and I believe that's true. That's why I love what Becca has created in this book. The 100-day journey will help you establish a healthy habit of choosing better thoughts and inviting Jesus to shape your perspective so that you can experience life to fullest."

Reed Moore, Lead Pastor Gwinnett Church

"Playing professional baseball for 15 years and now coaching the last 3, it's become clear the biggest separator between athletes is not a physical one, but mental! My dear friends Becca and Micah understand in order to fully live the lives we were created to live, to be the best version of ourselves, the true separator is in controlling the thoughts we feed our mind! I love the simplicity, the authenticity that these two share their hearts and their passion to lead others to become free and full of joy! Once you begin starting your day, choosing and thinking on life giving thoughts you'll realize the incredible opportunity you have through God's amazing grace and power, to begin changing your world for the better!"

Matt Tuiasosopo, Professional Baseball Player/
Head Coach Gwinnett Stripers

"The Lord blessed me when he sent Micah to my team. He and his family became family to me. They exemplify Jesus and lead by that great example. Micah was a great player and led us to a number 1 ranking, but more than his playing, he led our team through his example of loving Christ and living centered in that love. I will always thank God for sending me Micah as it made me a better coach and a better follower of Christ."

Charles Jones, Former Head Coach of Tulane Green Wave Baseball

ENDORSEMENTS AFTER READING BOOK 1, 2, OR 3

"Becca and her husband Dan have been a vital part of our church for years now. They have sharpened us with their wisdom, care and love. Much of how they do this is by teaching us how to think. As Becca points out, the choice to live life to the fullest is exactly that—a choice. And it starts with our minds. I believe the next 90 days will shape and elevate your thoughts. When this happens, with the help of Jesus, our lives elevate as well."

Jeff Henderson, Author of Know What You're FOR

"Becca helped me learn to see myself through God's eyes and not others or my own. Her gentle kindness and servant spirit for God shine through her as she pours her life and heart into others more than herself. This book is God's heart through her pen expressing the aspiration she has for all people, that they journey to a daily relationship with God, learn to love themselves the way that God loves them and, in turn, live their life to the fullest."

Josh Owings, CEO of Owings Enterprises LLC,
GA. State Director US Elite Baseball

"There is nothing worth fighting for more than the faith of the next generation. After spending years in student ministry, I came to the conclusion that there has never been a more challenging time to grow up than now. Countless things compete daily for our attention and slowly cause us to drift from the things that matter most. I have known Becca and her family for decades and have always respected their commitment to the next generation. Paul told us that we can be transformed by the renewal of our minds. I believe this book helps us to see what it looks like to practically tap into the power that Paul was talking about. This is a great resource that will strengthen your entire family."

Grant Partrick, Passion City Church Cumberland Location Pastor

"As we coach and care for the teenagers in our lives, not much is more important than encouraging them to practice renewing their minds. Becca's focus on spending a few moments each day to reflect on God's truth and focus on gratitude is a life changing practice not only for the young people who will build this habit, but also for the parents who are praying them through these tough years. I'm so excited for her to share these insights with a generation of kids who are hungry for them!"

Natalie Kitchen, North Point Leadership
Experience Residency Director

"I have been working witht middle school students for over 15 years; one of the main things I've seen is how students have so many negative thoughts hitting them, from friends, society, and even their own self-talk. What I love about this devotional from Becca is it trains you to start thinking positive thoughts about yourself, and giving yourself space to hear from God the positive thoughts he has to say about you, his child.

Al Causey, Gwinnett Church Family Ministries Director

"The concept of Living Life to the Fullest is a continuous process that we need to be reminded of often. As a parent, I believe it's life changing and important to instill in my life and my children's lives. As a teacher, I love this book and the message it's trying to get across to students. Too many people don't know how to live or experience life to the fullest. It's a lifelong process and skill! Without God, we are nothing!"

Dr. Natalie Gibson, Teacher, Mother, Leader in student ministry

"For as he thinks in his heart, so *is* he." (Proverbs 23:7 NKJV) I have read that we process over 50,000 thoughts each day, and 80% are negative! How do we learn to combat negative thinking, our diminished value to society, and build self-worth? *Choose Life to the Fullest* provides a daily framework to reinforce thankfulness, plant seeds of hope, offer and allow positive thoughts to shed light on shadows of doubt, and provide an Anchor for the Soul."

Jim Owings, Founder of Lord's Way Ministries

"God's heart for us all shines so beautifully through the words found in each devotional. Becca has humbly submitted her spirit, soul and body to declaring Gods truths in a simple, concise and easy to understand manner. The words cut through the chaos and distractions of life to refocus our minds, souls and spirits according to our true identity in Christ. Each devotional redirects our minds away from the lies of the enemy and this world back towards the truth, which can only come from right believing and a personal relationship with Jesus. I'm blessed to be ministered to by such a courageous, faithful servant of God."

Zenda Griebenow, Director and Tennis Coach

ENDORSEMENTS FROM STUDENTS

"Choose Life to the Fullest has changed the way I think throughout the day. Every time I start to get down or think negative thoughts I remember to change them and focus on what's good. I have been 100% happier and I enjoy life more after reading and applying this book."

Owin, 18, Baseball

"I believe our thoughts affect the way we live our life. Sometimes it's difficult to change our negative thoughts and think positive. *Choose Life to the Fullest* is very encouraging and includes amazing advice for shaping your thoughts."

Addi, 17, Basketball

"Having struggled through difficult feelings such as heartbreak, depression, and anxiety myself, this book reminded me that God has given us the ability to *choose* an abundant life, despite the hardships we face. I was reminded that feelings are not always truth, and feelings do *not* control us! Through reading this, I was encouraged to stand up to lies in practical ways."

Madison, College Student

"These daily devotions have impacted me emotionally and mentally. Whenever I feel like nothing can go my way. I think of the phrases and topics of the devotions and God always helps me power through it. All it takes is 5 minutes every day and I feel like a stronger person after."

Derek, 17, Baseball

"The 5 questions at the beginning of the devos help me to focus. Sometimes when I read the Bible, my mind will wander, but this is not the case with *Choose Life to the Fullest*. It helps me to actively align myself with what God will teach me that day. I face a lot at school and this may be the only positive word I receive all day."

JP, 17, Baseball and Crossfit

"I like them because they are short, powerful, and straight to the point. I get distracted and sleepy if people go on and on."

Toler, 13, Crossfit and Cross Country

"This devotional book is really making me think about Choosing Joy."

August, 12, Reading Harry Potter

"This is a fantastic devotional. I love the daily question. It really makes me think. This book helped me focus on casting aside fears and focusing on God."

Emily, 14, Riding horses

"This devotional starts my day off with positivity and the right attitude. It reminds me daily of God's love for me and the people He has blessed me with."

Ivan, 17, Basketball

"I woke up this morning and started thinking of 5 things I am thankful for."

Eben, 15, Tennis

"*Choose Life to the Fullest* provides truthful and encouraging reminders to start my day off with positivity and help me to focus on what is good. This devotional reminds me constantly of God's love for me and the many blessings He has placed in my life."

Claire, 16, Volleyball and Basketball

"I never thought about a lot of these questions until reading this book."

Pierce, 11, Baseball

"The 5 questions at the beginning of the lesson each day is what impacts me most, because it puts my focus on God and helps my day go better."

Christopher, 15, Basketball

"*Choose Life to the Fullest* has not just made an impact on the way I view myself, it has made a pivotal turn in my relationships with others. We can often start our day off on the wrong foot, but these daily devotionals have made a positive start to every day."

Savannah, 18, Spending time outdoors

Thank you...

Thankful to all the teenagers who previewed this book and gave their opinion.

Thankful for all of the encouragement in endorsements

Thankful to our family, Jim and Danise Owings, Dan Gunyon and each of the Gunyon kids,

Josh and Meredith Owings, Matt and Abi Tuiasosopo, JonMark Owings, and all our sweet nephews. What a blessing it is to be so close.

Thankful to Westbow Publishing for being so wonderful to work with.

Thankful to Lexie Fish for editing.

Thankful to Travis Fish for designing the cover.

Thankful to Gwinnett Church and Transit Team, Passion City Church, Free Chapel, and all the churches sharing the heart of Jesus

Thankful to Jesus, Who makes life to the fullest available to all!

INTRODUCTION...

When my *little* brother Micah (people always laugh when I introduce him as that because he is 6'5") was two or three years old he was watching a baseball game on TV when he decidedly said he was going to play major league baseball. Even as a little kid, he knew exactly what he wanted to do and was willing to work hard to make his dream a reality. Along the way he made intentional decisions to move him closer to his dream. He chose to practice, work hard, and have a good attitude.

From little league to middle school, then from high school state championships to college, and finally, Pros, I remember watching him pitch to players who were future hall of famers. I can also recall one amazing game where he hit two home runs over Turner field. What was especially fun is that he always invited us (his family) to be part of his dream.

Micah had a big dream and he chose repeatedly to work toward it—mentally, spiritually, physically, in every choice. Recently, he sent me this, "If we have the *choice* then what are those things that fuel or prompt us to *choose*? Maybe our desires, our goals, or the God-sized dream inside of us. It's one thing to say, "I want to be a better ball player," but simply choosing isn't going to make us better. It's the work we put in that makes us a better player." - MO

He asks, "What work or things can we apply to continue to enable us to CHOOSE God and the things He has for us?"

- What can we do today to move us closer to the goal or dream in our heart?
- What can we do spiritually?
- What can we do mentally?
- What can we do physically?
- What can we do to help someone else?

Answering these questions and doing something about it will lead us closer to our dreams and goals.

DAY 1

What is good in my life?

1.

2.

3.

4.

5.

"God can do anything, you know—far more than you could ever imagine or guess or request in your wildest dreams!" (Ephesians 3:20 MSG)

Big dreams can feel overwhelming! Some of us are afraid to really dream, because it feels unrealistic, unattainable or just too far away. But we can live out our dreams, even while we are pursuing them! In the introduction, I shared about my brother, Micah's dream. For him to reach his goals there was a long road. Yet, he was living his dream all along on the way, because he loved baseball and used every opportunity he had to play, work hard, and better himself.

Think about your dreams for a second. What can you do now to reach your goals?

What's stopping you from doing it?

For many of us, the "bigness" of our dream can make it feel out of our reach. We drag ourselves down by saying, "I might never reach my goals," or, "By the time I get there, what if I've changed my mind?" Going after the God-sized dream in our heart is life-giving. It makes ordinary days have purpose. Reaching a dream or a goal requires doing the little things over and over again day after day, and being faithful with the gifts, talents or hopes God has put in our heart.

We grew up outside the city, far from other houses or neighbors. On days when there was no organized practice or games, I remember Micah, as a little boy, hitting rocks with a bat to get some practice in.

One of my kids loves tennis. When the tennis courts got shut down during Covid we didn't want his dreams to feel shut down too, so my husband bought some big blocks of siding and set them against the side of the house so he could still practice.

There is always an opportunity for you to better yourself and work toward your goals. Sometimes, you just have to be creative to find it.

God, help me to stay motivated and to do the little things that will move me closer to my dreams. Give me the courage to chase after my dreams. In Jesus name

Who can I give life to today?

Five good things in my life are:

1.
2.
3.
4.
5.

"Jesus said, 'Love the Lord your God with ALL your person and prayer and intelligence. This is the most important, the first on any list.'"
(Matthew 6:37 MSG)

Life can feel so complex. Yet, so much in life is very simple. If everyday we just think, say, and do the next right thing in every area we can live life to the full! As a high school student I remember asking my youth pastor how to do the "right thing." He responded, "Love God, and love others. Then you'll always know what to do."

In every area of our lives we can ask ourselves, "Am I loving God in the way I _____ (date, think, talk, pursue my dreams, do homework, play my sport or activity, treat others, you fill in the blank)."

God knows us to the core of who we are and loves us there. He knows every detail, and nothing surprises Him. What He desires is that everyday we live in relationship with Him, just like we would a best friend.

Loving God means living your life constantly giving God your all and inviting Him into everything. When we do this He lives life in us and through us.

God, I invite You to live my moments with me. I give You me. In Jesus name

Who can I give life to today?

DAY 3

Five great things in my life:

1.
2.
3.
4.
5.

My youngest recently painted me a picture. To me, it's a treasure, a modern day Picasso. I believe God treasures our gifts to Him too. We may only see our mess ups or our imperfections, yet He sees our heart. He loves when we choose to give gifts to Him. Every word of encouragement, every act of kindness, every time we serve, every time we choose to pray instead of worry, every time we give joy, every time we share His heart, we give Him a gift.

What gift can I give to God?

The mystery of God amazes me, He fills our heart up with love and joy so we can give it away to others. The continual flow from

His heart to ours is like a stream. His stream of love never runs dry, but continues to fill our hearts so that we can spill Him out.

"For God SO loved the world." *(John 3:16 NIV)* This includes you, me, those we love, and those who are hard to get along with... for He *"so loved"* everyone!

God, may Your love continually flow into my heart so that Your love flows out on others. In Jesus name

Who can I give life to today?

DAY 4

What can I thank God for?

1.

2.

3.

4.

5.

"For if a man is in Christ he becomes a new person altogether—the past is finished and gone, everything has become fresh and new." (2 Corinthians 5:17 PHILIPS)

What if we lived everyday with the mindset that, "tomorrow is a new day!" The strike out left in the past. The missed opportunity no longer a big deal. The rejection no longer guiding our thoughts of self-doubt. All the negative from yesterday simply left in the past. Most of us chew on our mistakes, letting them roll around in our head causing us to wallow in regret. The enemy wants us to sit in yesterday's mess ups. God wants us to have hope for tomorrow.

When my brothers were playing ball, I watched them have both great days and hard days on the field. I asked Micah what he thought about this concept of letting yesterday go and living like tomorrow is a new day.

His response was:

I remember Dad telling me after tough games that tomorrow is another day and another opportunity! I think this was his way to encourage us to offer grace to ourselves (or others) instead of being bummed, being hard on ourselves, or having self-pity.

When we say "tomorrow is another day" we are changing our perspective from staying stuck in the hardships of today. We are enabling ourselves to learn from what happened, and move forward. All of the sudden we have an attitude of looking ahead to something, and our past failure is replaced by our present thought of future opportunity!

When you're able to grasp this simple phrase, you are turning a negative experience into a positive outlook. You cultivate motivation to make an improvement and be better. While you may have been knocked down, you're choosing to get up. - MO

How do we let go of yesterday? Give the disappointment, rejection, and bad memories to God and ask Him to replace it with His hope.

Jesus, here is my past, my yesterday's _____ (messups, struggles, memories of failure, rejection) I give this to You. Please replace it with Your hope. I choose to look forward to new opportunities today. In Your name

Who can I give life to today?

DAY 5

What things am I grateful for?

1.
2.
3.
4.
5.

"'Come,' he (Jesus) replied, 'and you will see.'" (John 1:39 NIV)

Come and see. So many times in the Bible Jesus invites us. This one word "come" is the invitation to experience the heart of God—His great love for us—and life to the full!

When He calls us, He is inviting us into a relationship with Him. So today as He asks us to come spend a few minutes in His presence. We can read a few verses in the Bible and see how they apply to us.

"Are you tired? Worn out? Burned out on religion? Come to me. Get away with me and you'll recover your life. I'll show you how to take a real rest. Walk with me and work with me—watch how I do it. Learn

the unforced rhythms of grace. I won't lay anything heavy or ill-fitting on you. Keep company with me and you'll learn to live freely and lightly."
(Matthew 11:28-30 MSG)

What does this verse mean to me?

Can I give God all of the things that are hurtful, stressful, or sad?

Jesus, I invite You into my life, I give You _____ (the things that make me feel tired and burned out) I accept Your invitation to come. Show me more of who You are. In Your name

Who can I give life to today?

DAY 6

Five good things in my life:

1.
2.
3.
4.
5.

"I can do ALL things through Him who strengthens me." (Philippians 4:13 KJV)

All of us face adversity, but what do you do with the adversity you face?

Dreams and sports are full of adversity and hard times, as well as amazing moments. Sometimes the adversity makes us want to quit, while those great moments fuel us to keep going. I wonder if it's what we do with adversity that gives us real strength and perseverance.

My brother Micah was amazing to watch as he pitched and hit home runs. But I also remember some difficult games. One night in Cincinnati as he played for the Reds, he had a hard night. We had traveled to see him with our young kids. After the game, he was walking in the parking lot all by himself and when he got into our minivan, I just knew it had been a night of adversity.

Micah's thoughts on adversity:

God's Word says adversity will happen and we will experience it. Philippians 4:13 is a common verse for athletes and many individual believers throughout the world. It's an easy one to remember and draw strength from.

Whether I was on the mound, at the plate, or during my intense training regime; I would find myself reciting this scripture under my breath or quietly saying it aloud (there is power in claiming God's Word out loud).

Often this verse comes to mind *'Greater is He that is in me, than he that is in the world' (1 John 4:4 KJV).* Over the years the Holy Spirit has spoken this further into my soul and told me, 'Micah my son, greater is HE (Christ) that is in me (Micah), than me (Micah) that is in this lost and broken world.' At this very moment, my perspective and outlook shifts to a reliance that is greater than my own. I am reminded every time how little my faith is, but how strengthened I am when I put it back in His Mighty Hands. My brothers and sisters, allow Him to be your strength and pull you through today! May God bless you and meet you where you are today! - MO

What will I do with the adversity I face?

How can I use scripture to be the positive reinforcement in my mind?

Jesus, I give you my heart and the pain I have felt from those hard moments of adversity. Help me to remember that when I am weak, You are strong, and You will empower me as I rely on You. In Jesus name

Who can I give life to today?

DAY 7

What is good in my life?

1.
2.
3.
4.
5.

Thoughts from Micah:

Due to this being so prevalent in today's age and throughout the history of mankind, I wanted to dig a little deeper on the topic of adversity.

If you google search the definition of adversity, this is what comes up, "Difficulties, misfortune, bad luck, trouble, hardship, distress, disaster, suffering, affliction, sorrow, misery, heartbreak, tribulation, woe, trauma, torment, mishap, torture, setback, crisis, tragedy, trial, tribulation." (dictionary.com)

Man, it's tough to read through all those negative words. If you look closely the majority of them involve something happening to you. I mentioned yesterday that God's Word says we will experience adversity or struggles, so it's not a question of *if* we will, but *when*. When we do, what do we do? The apostle Paul writes to the Romans, *"We also have joy with our troubles (suffering or adversity), because we know these troubles produce patience. And patience produces character, and character produces hope. And this hope will never disappoint us, because God has poured out his love to fill our hearts. He gave His love through the Holy Spirit, whom God has given to us."* (Romans 5:3-5 NCV)

I'm addressing this to you, dreamers and athletes, because it largely applies to life itself. I have been in your shoes…I've struck out with the bases loaded when the game is on the line. I've thrown the ball down the middle of the plate and paid for it. I've booted the routine ground ball and dropped the easy pop fly. I've had injuries and setbacks. Worst of all, I've felt the weight of the world on my shoulders and heaviness in my heart by letting my teammates, loved ones, and God down.

I've felt that pressure through adversity and troubles. I can't sit here and tell you that I always had *"joy with my troubles,"* but I can tell you that I learned patience and resilience. I'm still learning! I can tell you that I gained character and lots of hope. The hope God makes available to us and breathes into our hearts will fuel you and ignite your innermost being. It will give you a resolve to encourage you to get through and you will succeed! You'll win because He has already won and wants you to have victories too! - MO

What adversity am I facing?

Can I believe that with God, I will experience victory over this?

Jesus, I invite You into my adversity. I need Your hope and joy to overcome this. In Your name

Who can I give life to today?

DAY 8

Five good things in my life:

1.
2.
3.
4.
5.

"And he will be called, Wonderful Counselor, Mighty God, Everlasting Father, Prince of Peace." (Isaiah 9:6 NIV)

Looking a little closer, what does this verse say about Jesus. A wonderful counselor does a few things:

- Creates a safe place to be real.
- Listens intently.
- Gently helps us discover and face truth.
- Enters our pain with us.
- Equips us with a plan to grow toward health.
- Speaks wise truth.
- Laughs with us and cries with us.
- Takes us by the hand, leading us to a place of healing.

These are a few characteristics of a good counselor, but Jesus is the *Wonderful* Counselor. Living in relationship with Jesus gives us even more, we are given the gift of His unconditional, powerful, tender love to fill our hearts. This wows me.

As we move toward Jesus, may we be aware of Who He is and may we go to Him with our real stuff.

Jesus, show me how to sit with You and be real. I give you permission to enter into my disappointments and pain, and lead me to wisdom in all areas in my life. In Your name

Who can I give life to today?

DAY 9

Five things I am grateful for:

1.
2.
3.
4.
5.

"And he will be called, Wonderful Counselor, Mighty God, Everlasting Father, Prince of Peace." (Isaiah 9:6 NIV)

We talked about what a Wonderful Counselor Jesus is, but what does a "Mighty God" look like?

- He is the Creator of all life. He made waterfalls, sunrises, mountaintops, and every creature on the earth. HE also made us: our body, our mind, our soul, our heart.
- He makes miracles of healing and life change.
- He rescues us by beating death and sin.

Jesus is the God who loves us beyond comprehension. He came here and put on skin—just to be with us! We can look at our circumstances and we can feel lost, overwhelmed, even desperate, or we can look around and realize God is Mighty and His fingerprints are everywhere. His power knows no limits. He is here. He rescues us. He saves us. He loves ALL of His creation, which includes us.

As we look around today, let's look closer, deeper and realize life is much bigger than our circumstances. We can come to the Mighty King Jesus and He will give us life to the full!

Do I forget how mighty God is?

Jesus, I invite You into my day, my thoughts, my moments, my fears, my unknowns, my relationships, my feelings, my future. I give You me. In Your name

Who can I give life to today?

DAY 10

Five things I enjoy:

1.
2.
3.
4.
5.

"And he will be called, Wonderful Counselor, Mighty God, Everlasting Father, Prince of Peace." (Isaiah 9:6 NIV)

Jesus says *"Come to Me."* Who is this Jesus who invites us into a relationship with Him? We have been looking at this verse in Isiah to give us an idea about *Who* we are coming to.

As we think about the "Everlasting Father," what does this aspect of Jesus' character mean for us?

"If you took the love of all the best mothers and fathers who have lived in the course of human history, all their goodness, kindness, patience, fidelity, wisdom, tenderness, strength, and love and united all those qualities in a single person, that person's love would only be a faint shadow of the furious love and mercy in the heart of God the Father addressed to you and me at this moment." (Brennan Manning, The Furious Longing of God)

The love of Jesus reaches past our insecurities and loves us in our brokenness and failures. God's continual love displayed in the life of Jesus is tender, powerful, never-ending, all-consuming, unconditional. His love silences the voices in my mind that say I should be more, do more, have more...and loves me completely.

Do I live basing my identity on the truth that I am loved completely by the God of the Universe?

If not, Why?

Jesus, I give You me. I choose Your love and Your heart—let this become my identity. Everlasting Father, comfort and heal the brokenness in my life. In Your name

Who can I give life to today?

What is good in my life?

1.
2.
3.
4.
5.

"Because He bends down and listens, I will pray as long as I breathe!"
(Psalms 116:2 TLB)

Part 1 on prayer from Micah:

In your sport or dream (whatever you do that is life-giving to you), how does prayer become part of your routine?

I'm thankful that my sister asked me this question because I had never thought about it before. Though I can't fully explain the process of how prayer became part of my overall preparation for the game, I believe in part it was due to being raised in a loving Christian home that included prayer throughout our days.

Growing up I was around some incredible men who instilled in me the importance to pray before the game. Usually there is someone in most youth and amateur teams who take it upon themselves to rally a group of players who want to participate in praying together prior to going to battle with each other and themselves (physically and mentally). I say this because I was a part of doing so for the majority of my amateur career. Oftentimes this would take place down the foul line, and instead of anyone being put on the spot to pray, the whole group would recite the Lord's Prayer (Matthew 6:9-13) while kneeling together. In the midst of this moment, there is a connection with your teammates and brothers that far transcends playing with each other on the field. There is also a moment when nothing else is on your mind (worries, anxiety, doubt, fear, clutter, etc). The attention and focus is on our Father in Heaven, who loves each one of us!

Our quiet whispers, our anxious thoughts, our broken sentences, our music, our calling on Him, our prayer and our entire being summons the heart of God. - MO

How can I make prayer a daily routine?

Jesus, thank You for always listening to me. Here are my thoughts, my needs, my hopes, my worries _____ (list them out if you need to). I invite You into every area of my life. In Your name

Who can I give life to today?

What five things am I thankful for?

1.
2.
3.
4.
5.

"This is how you should pray: 'Our Father in heaven, hallowed be your name your kingdom come, your will be done, on earth as it is in heaven. Give us today our daily bread. And forgive us our debts, as we also have forgiven our debtors And lead us not into temptation, but deliver us from the evil one.'" (Matthew 6:9-13 NIV)

Part 2 on prayer from Micah:

Yesterday I mentioned the Lord's Prayer and how it's often recited before games. I love this prayer because it's how Jesus taught us to pray. As my young adult playing days progressed into high school, college and beyond, many of my team continued to join together and pray before the game and sometimes me or another teammate would pray over our group.

Typically, the National Anthem is played before games in high school and college sports. While the Anthem was being played, I began to find this time very special and used it to pray for the health and well being of those in the game and my individual performance, that God would empower me to display the abilities He blessed me with to the fullest.

As my pro career got underway, I kept praying for the above, but I also began praying for my family and loved ones, that God would watch over them, protect them, meet them where they were, and love on them. During this time I felt connected to my Father in Heaven and my family back home, even though I was often thousands of miles away from my family and friends.

May we remember the power of prayer and believe that God hears us, is with us, and for us! Oftentimes I picture He's sitting with a smile on his face as He listens with an intentional and engaged look as I talk with Him! - MO

What can I pray about today?

Have I ever thought about God smiling at me? Why or why not?

Jesus, I invite You into my day, my dreams, my future, my good thoughts and my anxious thoughts. I give You me. In Your name

Who can I give life to today?

What can I thank God for?

1.
2.
3.
4.
5.

"Pray continually." *(1 Thessalonians 5:17 NIV)*

Part 3 on prayer from Micah:

During my career I learned to establish a routine and stick with it. Oftentimes this included eating the same pre-game meal prior to my evening start. Once I got to the field, the routine I had was planned out to the minute.

As my professional career began, and the subsequent promotion to higher levels, I started to realize I needed to be more intentional about my prayer life and include prayer in my routine. Not just to check the box, I felt the conviction that praying should be included in my preparation before the game. I don't remember exactly how it came about it or started, but one day I asked my sister if she would pray with me before my game. If you know Becca then you know she, of course, said yes.

For four to five years I called Becca before every game. It became part of my routine. I remember slipping away from my locker to different spots in the clubhouse—for home games in Arizona, that spot was always in the laundry area where our uniforms were stored. They had a big ol' comfy recliner I'd always sit in. On the road, it might be in the tunnel or dugout, or, at times, I'd just put a towel over my head and call from my locker.

These calls to pray with my sister an hour and twenty minutes before game time were very special to me. Becca was always on standby, ready and waiting, and that was even while she had multiple kids under ten at home! A lot of times it was close to the kid's bedtime on the east coast, but she always took the time to pray with me. It was during these 3-5 minutes that we would come before our Heavenly Father and give Him the game I was about to have the opportunity and joy to play. Becca's calm, peaceful voice helped ease the adrenaline that was starting to boil as I prepared to go out to pitch on center stage in front of huge crowds, oftentimes upwards of 50,000.

I believe routine is important in every player's career and in each person's life. Why? Because it's a place of comfort. Things come along that are unexpected and we have to adjust, but the routine helps us stay the course and removes a lot of the stress and pressure we might otherwise face. Routines help us feel prepared. After praying with Becca before games I knew I was ready to go out, have fun, and be free to do the best I could! I was ready for the battle because I wasn't alone. By inviting God into my games and asking His (not mine) power to be shown, He was able to do some amazing things on the diamond through me for many to witness!

I thank Becca for the prayer time and God for that dream of mine coming true and pray that yours will too! Remember to invite Him in and consider developing a routine that includes spending time talking with our precious Father above! - MO

Is there someone I can pray with regularly?

Could I invite this person into my dreams and goals by praying with them?

Jesus, I invite You into every area of my life. In Your name

Who can I give life to today?

I am thankful for:

1.
2.
3.
4.
5.

"For God so loved the world." (John 3:16 NIV)

Life is made up of moments. Moments determine our hours. Hours make up our day. Days become our months. Months turn into years. If we stop and think about it, we can see where we want to be in a few years from now. To get there we must ask ourselves, "Am I doing the things (mentally, physically, spiritually) in the moments I'm given that will get me to where I want to go?"

As I read *Chase the Lion,* by Mark Batterson, I underlined so many of his words. He has great wisdom for those pursuing a dream. He says, "This could be the greatest year of your life, your dream year, but you have to win the day. That's how you win the week, win the month, win the year. No one achieves his or her dream without daily disciplines."

We can ask ourselves:

- What can I do today to get myself where I want to go?
- What can I read today to train my mind to stay motivated?
- What can I do today to improve myself?

To live moments to the fullest, we must embrace the truth that God loves us with an unconditional powerful tender healing motivating love. His love fuels us, whereas our own negative thoughts can defeat us.

Jesus, I invite You into my moments, my thoughts, my goals and my dreams. Help me to live one moment at a time moving closer to what You have placed in my heart. In Jesus name

Who can I give life to today?

Five great things in my life:

1.
2.
3.
4.
5.

"Summing it all up, friends, I'd say you'll do best by filling your minds and meditating on things true, noble, reputable, authentic, compelling, gracious—the best, not the worst." (Philippians 4:8 MSG)

Dreamers and athletes need a "go to" thought. A go to thought is a one that carries us during stressful moments when our brain wants to go negative or when the enemy tries to discourage us. A go to thought is one of the most powerful tools we can use in stressful situations. If our brain tries to pull us in a downward spiral, we can tell it to stop and reroute our brain to think something different.

Some good go to thoughts are:

- God has great things for me.
- I am a masterpiece in Christ Jesus.
- My identity comes from being God's child.
- I am a champion.
- I am a conqueror.
- I am a treasure.

Switching our focus can actually switch the outcome of a stressful moment. Thinking something great can make something great happen.

What do I think most of the time?

What can I choose to be my "go to" thought?

Jesus, I invite You into my thoughts. Help me to focus on the best, not the worst. In your name

Who can I give life to today?

What five things are good in my life?

1.
2.
3.
4.
5.

What do I think about most of the time?

Do I think about the things that are good in my life?

"If you are really wise, you'll think this over—it's time you appreciated God's deep love." (Psalms 107:43 MSG)

"The secret conversations you hold in the privacy of your own mind are shaping your destiny, little by little. With every thought that races through your mind, you are continually reinventing yourself and your future. Research indicates the average person thinks 50,000 thoughts a day. This is either good news or bad news because every thought moves you either toward your God-given potential or away from it. NO thoughts are neutral." (Tommy Newberry, Living a Joy Filled Life)

Words from Micah:

Can you believe we have over 50 *thousand* thoughts in a day? WOW! At times, I'm guilty of allowing negative or bad thoughts affect my attitude.

It's been proven that it takes 21 days to break a habit. Sometimes, to reach a big goal, you have to do it in small increments at a time. So, what if you just committed to doing a devo each morning for the next 21 days? That's doable, right?

You already wrote down five good things in your life, but I want to take it a step further and ask you to write three words (joy, faith, love, endure, blessed, whatever you want!) on your hand with a sharpie, or on a sticky note somewhere you'll see it everyday like your bathroom mirror.

When you get down on yourself or a negative thought creeps in, look down at your hand! Trust me, it helps! - MO

Jesus, I invite You into my thoughts, I give You my mind and heart. In Your name

Who can I give life to today?

DAY 17

What are my five thankfuls?

1.
2.
3.
4.
5.

"Immense in mercy and with an incredible love, he embraced us."
(Ephesians 2:4 MSG)

Thoughts from Micah:

Have you ever wondered why the hardest person to love is yourself.
I can love others and believe God loves them, but sometimes it's
hard to believe God loves me.

Why do we feel this way? I think it's because we know ourselves
better than anyone else knows us (except God). We know about
our thoughts, our selfish desires, and our darkest moments. We
know what we did last night or last year.

The good thing is God knows all of this too and God is not in love with some future version of you. He's in love with you as you are right now! God is able to see through the struggles we have and our sins, and continue to love and pursue us.

God, help me to see me as you see me. Help me see and feel Your love for me. Help me love myself! May I keep pursuing You, Father, as You pursue me. In Jesus name

Who can I give life to today?

DAY 18

What is good in my life?

1.
2.
3.
4.
5.

Words from Micah:

"'Because you have so little faith. Truly I tell you, if you have faith as small as a mustard seed, you can say to this mountain, 'Move from here to there,' and it will move. Nothing will be impossible for you.'" (Matthew 17:20 NIV)

Did you catch that? If you have the faith of a mustard seed, then nothing and *no thing* is impossible for you.

How big do you think your faith is?

Do you believe in Jesus? That He died and rose for you, that He's with you and for you? Faith is a choice, not a feeling! And you can choose it today, it's simple! - MO

We can choose faith every day by inviting Jesus in!

Jesus, I give You me. I choose to believe that You died and rose for me. I invite You into every area of my life. Purify my heart and forgive me. in Your name

Who can I give life to today?

What is good in my life?

1.
2.
3.
4.
5.

"Thank God no matter what happens." (1 Thessalonians 5:17 MSG)

Words from Micah:

Oftentimes we get so caught up in what's going on around us, or what we are looking forward to, we forget to look back at where we came from, what we endured to get to where we currently are, and God's continued faithfulness. During my career I took great delight in thinking back about where my love for the game came from and all those that made an impact along the way. One of my fondest memories is playing catch with my dad in the yard. As a young child, I know this is where God planted the love of the game inside me. All throughout my playing career, Dad would put a glove on and toss with me. It was our thing and we continued to do it as long as I played. During difficult times throughout the season, I remembered playing catch with my Dad and it helped keep me grounded in loving what I had the opportunity to do.

Some people don't realize the things athletes go through to get to the top. They just see pro athletes as fortunate or lucky. While there is a lot of truth to this, there is also a lot of work, discipline, sacrifice, dedication, pain, and unknowns to push through along the journey. I was empowered to keep pushing and know that I was better because of my dedication, relentless grinding, and overcoming.

God's faithfulness was there the entire time. Even when I doubted or had little faith in where I was, what role I had, why I got demoted, and even through injuries and other setbacks. Answers to a lot of those questions we dwell on is not always necessary. God's faithfulness that He is ALWAYS with us must be remembered! - MO

Jesus, remind me of your goodness, I invite you into every area of my life today. In your name

Who can I give life to today?

DAY 20

What am I thankful for today?

1.
2.
3.
4.
5.

"You've heard me tell you, 'I'm going away, and I'm coming back.' If you loved me, you would be glad that I'm on my way to the Father because the Father is the goal and purpose of my life." (John 14:28 MSG)

Words from Micah:

There is an acronym I use, PLIYL. It means, "Play like it's your last!" I would write this in every locker I used. Even on the road, one of the first things I'd do when I got to the stadium was tear off some athletic tape from the trainers room and write out this statement in my locker where I could see it throughout the day.

At different times during my career I'd sharpie PLIYL on my hand. For me, this phrase put things in perspective. It motivated me to work hard that day and give it my best! Reading and reciting it would often help me settle my heart and mind and relieve any tensions I might have been dealing with internally.

The other thing it did for me was remind me of the opportunity I had. How many thousands of kids had dreamed of putting on a Big League uniform? I wasn't sitting behind a desk at a computer, (although there is nothing wrong with a desk job) I was getting to lace up spikes and get dirty for a living! This phrase helped me to always remember what I had and be grateful for every moment.

PLIYL should encourage you and free you to go out and have FUN being on the field, or doing what you love, because there are so many people who wish they could do what you get to do. Take pride in that. Take JOY in approaching the game or practice like it could be your last! - MO

What would change if we lived like every moment was our last time to do that thing we love?

How would this change our perspective?

What can I thank God for?

Jesus, I invite you into my moments. Help me to live each moment to the fullest!

In Jesus name

Who can I give life to today?

What am I thankful for?

1.
2.
3.
4.
5.

"But the Holy Spirit produces this kind of fruit in our lives: love, joy, peace, patience, kindness, goodness, faithfulness, gentleness, and self-control. There is no law against these things!" (Galatians 5:22 NLT)

Focusing on one, positive word can be super motivating and speak to the negative thoughts we think. We can do this during any season of life and in any sport, hobby, ministry, work, relationship and all life situations we are in.

About five years ago, my kids told me that I was joyful and loving, but NOT peaceful. This was after a sermon where our pastor at Gwinnett Church talked about embracing and owning one fruit of the spirit of a year.

Peace became my word. Peace became my goal. Peace became the gift I wanted to give others. Peace became who I wanted to be.

It took me more than a year to get peaceful...maybe three years and, at times, I still struggle to be peaceful.

When you own a word, it becomes part of your world. Study it. Research it. Write it everywhere. Notice other people who possess this quality. If you aren't sure what your word should be, ask God to reveal it to you.

What do you struggle with?

What is the opposite of this struggle? (This might be your word.)

What word can you pick and own for the rest of the year?

Jesus, I invite You into my mind, my heart, my disappointment, my struggles, my hopes, my future, my relationships. Give me a word that would help me grow this year and bless those around me. In Your name

Who can I give life to today?

What is good in my life?

1.
2.
3.
4.
5.

"We destroy arguments and every lofty opinion raised against the knowledge of God, and take every thought captive to obey Christ." (2 Corinthians. 10:5 ESV)

"First, think. Second, believe. Third, dream. And finally, dare." (Walt Disney)

Our first thoughts of the day shape our belief system, and we live this out everyday. If we think about the great, we will live great, regardless of our situation. Thinking about the good is a choice that can change your life. For most of us, it's our bend to think about what we're not, where we fail, how we measure up to others, our faults, gaps and areas of improvements. But God has so much more for us. He wants us to take *every* thought captive.

That means taking those negative, self-defeating thoughts and sending them away. One of the most powerful ways to do this is to change a bad thought into a good one. When we do this, by wrapping God's truth around it, we have something bigger than ourselves to put our identity in.

Micah and I have been talking about picking a word or phrase that becomes your motivation. Sometimes before we can fully do this, we have to acknowledge the negative thoughts that beat us up day after day. God has more for us. *"I have loved you with an everlasting love; I have drawn you with unfailing kindness." (Jeremiah 31:3 NIV).* *"I (God) have written your name on the palms of my hands." (Jeremiah 49:16 NLT).*

God loves us so much that He writes our names on His hands. When we embrace and own that we are lovable to God and that we can put our identity in His love instead of our performance, the scoreboard, winning the game, getting an A, being popular, looking a certain way, achieving the promotion, life change happens!

We get to choose our thoughts! We can choose to beat ourselves up in our mind, which defeats us or, to remind ourselves of the identity God has for us.

Jesus, I invite You into everything. Take my self-defeating thoughts. I choose to accept that You made me and You love me, help this to become my identity. May I live this out in the things I love to do. In Jesus name

Who can I give life to today?

DAY 23

What is great in my life?

1.
2.
3.
4.
5.

"And now I entrust you to God and the message of his grace that is able to build you up and give you an inheritance with all those he has set apart for himself." (Acts 20:32 NLT)

If we wake up every morning and think positively about our day, regardless of our situation something great will happen! Even on those worst days, we can wake up and think, "Today is going to be great!" That is one of the first things I tell myself in the morning because I know that our thoughts jumpstart our brain and shape our day!

My brother-in-law, Matt Tuiasosopo, played baseball professionally and now coaches in the Braves organization. He works with my son, Owin, and has given him great advice.

Matt told me this about going through slumps:

All athletes regardless of the sport go through slumps. The key is not necessarily avoiding them but limiting the amount of time spent in them. How quickly can you snap out of it. How can you prolong the mountain peak moments and how short can you keep the time in the valleys. It is through overcoming the battle of the mind. That is what separates the good players from the great ones. Great players, mentally strong athletes, because of their consistency in how they mentally prepare and fill their minds with what is true and excellent, do not stay down in the valley long. That is why it never seems like they ever struggle. Maybe a slump lasts for a few games or a week, but hardly ever does it last weeks or months or for a full season. They have mentally figured out how to stay positive, confidant, and focused on the process, despite poor results because they know who they are and what they do. By placing your identity in Christ and believing you are who He says you are, you allow yourself to be at peace and play freely without fear. You understand a bad day is just that, a bad day. Tomorrow is a new day and a great opportunity to go be great! - MT-

What do you do when you are in a slump?

Have you ever thought that your negative thoughts about yourself can keep you in a slump? But you don't have to stay there. You get to choose your thoughts about yourself, your relationships, your everyday life, your sport or dream, and how God feels about you. If you play out of the truth that you have worth and value because you are made and loved by God, you will thrive and your slumps will be short-lived.

Jesus, I trust Your heart for me I choose to. Even when it doesn't feel like it's going to be a great day, I choose to believe You are for me and You are working something great! In Your name

Who can I give life to today?

DAY 24

What is good in my life?

1.
2.
3.
4.
5.

"The fruit of the Spirit is love, joy, peace, patience, kindness, goodness, faithfulness, gentleness, self-control; against such things there is no law." (Galatians 5:22-23 ESV)

Words from Micah:

Control the controllables. These three words began making a huge impact in my career and life when I was 24 years old. To this day, I'm still reminded of how important it is to control the controllables. While I don't play professional baseball anymore, being able to focus on what I can control has greatly impacted my life, relationships, and walk with Jesus.

Control takes action on our part: to run, direct, have authority over, drive, to be in charge of.

I encourage you to make a list of the things you can't control and a list of the things you can control. First write down things that relate to your sport, dream or hobby. If you play a sport it might be where you play, when you play, who you play with, calls made by the referees, or decisions your coaches make. Then write down things that apply to your everyday life. There are a lot of things in life we can't control. There are many more things out of your control from the weather, to what teacher you have, to if your parents get divorced. Remember, focusing on what you *can* control is a practice that, over time, eventually becomes a habit. - MO

What can I control?

What can't I control?

How can I give the second list to God?

Facing the things in our life that might be difficult or out of our control is hard sometimes, but it's also empowering and creates an environment where we can initiate changes.

God, there are a lot of things I can't control in life. Please forgive me for any bitterness or anger I feel about things that have been out of my control. I choose to invite You into life's disappointments. Please give me Your peace and strength for the things I can't control, and the wisdom to choose wisely for the things I can control. I invite You to help me think great even when life is not going my way. In Jesus name

Who can I give life to today?

What am I grateful for?

1.
2.
3.
4.
5.

"I thank you, Lord, with all my heart." (Psalms 38:1 GNT)

Words from Micah:

Let our focus turn to what we CAN control. Again, this takes practice, it won't be an overnight miracle. Once we define the things we can control, we replace our focus on them instead of the things we can't control.

I had some really good teammates in my career. Early on, I remember getting so worked up when they would make a mistake. My attention remained on the error my teammate made and would affect my focus on my own game. As my career progressed I began looking at that particular infielder who made an error, tapping my glove and saying, "I got you, I'll get us out of this." The shift in mindset enabled me to re-channel my focus on what I could control, which was the next pitch.

Other things we can control:

- How I train and prepare,
- My diet,
- My approach at the plate,
- My reaction to calls or decisions I don't agree with,
- How I treat others,
- Who I hang out with (others that make me better or wrong crowd that brings me down),
- My attitude,
- My effort,
- Discipline to read, pray, journal,
- How I manage my time,
- How hard I work, and
- Serving others and making an effort to help. - MO

Jesus, I invite You into my thoughts and my day. Remind me of what I can control. In Your name

Who can I give life to today?

What can I thank God for?

1.
2.
3.
4.
5.

"'If you'll hold on to me for dear life,' says God, 'I'll get you out of any trouble. I'll give you the best of care, if you'll only get to know and trust me. Call me and I'll answer.'" (Psalms 91:14-16 MSG)

We can overcome those hard days! For the last two days Micah talked about things we can't control, and things we can control. How can we overcome and move forward when life throws us things that are out of our control?

There are two things we can do with the things we can't control and disappointments we face. First, we can give them to God. When we do this, great healing happens! When we invite Jesus into our pain, hard times, or disappointments, he provides an answer to us. Second, we can hold on to God every day by praying, which is simply talking to him like a friend. When we read in the Bible, the words can actually feel like they're coming alive! That's how He talks back to us. Today's scripture reminds us to hold on to Him.

Everyday, we can choose to be thankful. Today, despite the unknowns, we can find something to express gratitude for. We can tell God we want to hold onto him by inviting Jesus into our thoughts, dreams, hopes, goals, relationships, everything!

Some great places to read in the bible about what it means to hold onto God are the books of John, Psalms, and 1 and 2 Timothy.

We can overcome when we invite God's power into our lives!

God, I give You _____ that I can't control. I'm going to hold onto You, I give You me. I choose to trust You when I'm nervous and with all the things I can't control. May Your power protect and provide for me. In Jesus name

Who can I give life to today?

What is good in my life?

1.
2.
3.
4.
5.

"The Lord replied, 'My Presence will go with you, and I will give you rest.' Then Moses said to him, 'If your Presence does not go with us, do not send us up from here. How will anyone know that you are pleased with me and with your people unless you go with us? What else will distinguish me and your people from all the other people on the face of the earth?' And the Lord said to Moses, 'I will do the very thing you have asked, because I am pleased with you and I know you by name.' Then Moses said, 'Now show me your glory.'" (Exodus 33:14-18 NIV)

I love this dialogue that Moses is having with the Lord. A few key words that jump out to me are, presence, rest, distinguished, pleased, name, and glory. Over the next couple days, Becca and I will dive deeper into this! Know that God is with you, for you, and loves you! - MO

If I could see God what would I talk to him about?

What do I think He would tell me?

God, I believe You are with me, start speaking to me through
Your words in the Bible and when I pray help me to learn how
to hear You in my thoughts. In Jesus name

Who can I give life to today?

What is good in my life?

1.
2.
3.
4.
5.

Thoughts from Micah:

Moses asked God, *"What else will distinguish me and your people from all the other people on the face of the earth?"* *(Exodus 33:16 NIV)*

Just think about that. Moses wanted to know what exactly sets him and God's people apart from everyone else. Do you ever ask yourself what distinguishes you from your peers? Though being a Christian might be hard or uncool at times, it's also really motivating to know that you are set apart because of your faith.

Back in high school, I made a commitment to my parents that I wouldn't drink even a sip of alcohol, do any sort of drugs, or have sex during my entire high school career. In exchange, my parents would send me on a graduation trip to anywhere in the world I wanted to go! My folks did this with my brothers and sisters too.

As I sit here and write, I remember how hard it was at times because the majority of my friends (sometimes it felt like everyone at my school besides me) were participating in at least one of these activities. I wanted to fit in and be "cool," but I found out that I was actually respected for the decisions I was making.

My reasoning for not going down that road began as a promise to my parents, because I wanted to honor them and myself (and I also wanted to go to Hawaii). As high school continued, my choices were also fed by the desire to be distinguished and respected from my peers and their parents. I was also very serious about my future baseball career and I knew drinking or drugs weren't going to aid me in my path to success.

It wasn't always easy to be set apart. There were parties I missed out on, there were times when I was teased or made fun of, but high school is short and I don't regret my decisions to stay clean and stay on track.

As I continue to seek to be distinguished I'm reminded that I must first seek God. *"But seek first his kingdom and his righteousness, and all these things will be given to you as well." (Matthew 6:33 NIV)* - MO

Do those around me notice something different about me?

Am I distinguished in my faith?

What is there to lose by making the promise to stay away from things I know aren't going to help me on my path to success?

What is there to gain by making the promise to make the right choices?

Jesus, Help me to live distinguished in my faith. Give me the courage to follow in your footsteps and stay away from what could harm me.

Who can I give life to today?

DAY 29

What is good in my life:

1.
2.
3.
4.
5.

Yesterday MO talked about being distinguished in our faith. Early this morning God started whispering to me, *"Faith? Or fear?"* You have a choice. To be distinguished and set apart in our faith, we have to risk, trust, and choose faith over our fears.

"Give your entire attention to what God is doing right now, and don't get worked up about what may or may not happen tomorrow. God will help you deal with whatever hard things come up when the time comes." (Matthew 6:34 MSG)

We can choose faith, because of these truths about God:

- God loves us.
- He sent Jesus to deliver us from sin and struggle.

- We can make a choice to put our trust in Jesus (His life, death, and resurrection).
- We can invite the life-changing power of Jesus into our lives.
- Nothing can separate us from God's love (Romans 8).

We can choose to live in faith even if we don't feel like it. We put our trust in Jesus, which may feel like a risk, yet it will change everything in amazing ways and give us the courage to live distinguished in our faith.

Why can we trust God even during the most difficult times?

Jesus, I believe YOU are for me, You died for me, You rose again. I choose to trust You, even when I don't feel like it. I invite Your love and power into my life. In Your name

Who can I give life to today?

What in my life is fun?

1.
2.
3.
4.
5.

"I (Jesus) have come that they may have life, and have it to the full."
(John 10:10 NIV)

The theme of Choose Life to the Fullest books came from a sketch my teenage daughter made for me. "Life to the *FULLEST*." This framed quote sits by the entryway of our home, reminding me daily to ask myself:

- Am I living my best life?
- Am I giving life to others?
- Do I share the heart of Jesus by the way I interact with others?

Jesus came so we can live life to the fullest! We don't have to walk around empty, searching, wondering, or longing. He fills our heart with His great love, so we can live our life enjoying each moment and giving life to others.

If you haven't picked a phrase, quote, or verse to motivate you in this season, I encourage you to! Today's verse is a great one to get you through every day. Writing scripture out has power. Putting your word or phrase somewhere where you can see it reminds you to always live your best life. "Life to the FULLEST." This is my prayer for you!

Am I living life to the fullest?

In what ways can I give life to those around me?

How can I show Jesus' love in the way I live my life?

Jesus, I give You me. Remind me constantly that YOU have life to the full for me. Help me to live in a way where your love overflows in my world and gives life to others. In Your name

Who can I give life to today?

Five great things in my life:

1.
2.
3.
4.
5.

"Look at me (Jesus). I stand at the door. I knock. If you hear me call and open the door, I'll come right in." (Revelations 3:20 MSG)

If Jesus came to the door of your house and knocked on the door, what would you do? How would you feel? Would you be excited or nervous? What would you want to ask Him?

Every day we end with a prayer to invite Jesus in. He wants to be invited into every area of our life! We were created to do life with Him. He knows that if we shut Him out, we will walk around empty and unfulfilled. In the beginning when human beings were created, we were created for a relationship with God.

Even though we can't see Jesus with our eyes, we can invite Him into every aspect of our lives. When we do this something mysterious happens and His Spirit comes to do life with us! His Spirit fills us on the inside. What would change if we invited the presence and power of Jesus into our moments, our thoughts, and every interaction that we have?

For me this would mean waking up and inviting Jesus into my time with Him, my exercise routine, my conversations with my family, my drive on the way to school and work, my thoughts on how to care for others, my meetings, my moments of brainstorming, dinner time, what I do with my free time, and my thoughts before I go to sleep.

Could you try this for 24 hours? One day at a time, choose to invite God into your life and see how he guides your path and grows your faith.

Jesus, I invite You into this conversation, this class or meeting, this moment with my friends, my routine, my plan, the chores I do, my hopes, the things that swirl in my head, I invite You into *everything*. In Your name

Who can I give life to today?

DAY 32

Five good things in my life:

1.
2.
3.
4.
5.

"Come to me, all you who are weary and burdened, and I will give you rest. Take my yoke upon you and learn from me, for I am gentle and humble in heart, and you will find rest for your souls. For my yoke is easy and my burden is light." (Matthew 11:28-30 NIV)

Thoughts from Micah:

What do you think about when you hear the word "rest?" The majority of us think about sleeping, taking a nap, or relaxing on the couch.

To rest in the Lord means that we declare something is finished. We read in Genesis where God created the Heaven and Earth, and on the seventh day He rested. Too often we look at that and think that God rested because He was tired, but does God even get tired? I don't think so. God rested and was at peace because His work was complete!

Have you ever worked on something with such concentration for so long that when you finished, you heave this huge sigh of relief? It could be a big test or paper in school, an important competition or game, even mowing the lawn or a project around the house.

I remember being so focused and locked-in during some of my games afterwards I would need to sit down at my locker and just take a deep breath. The game was over, it was finished. If that's how I felt after a baseball game, I wonder how God felt on the day after creating the Heavens and Earth!

He provides us rest, peace, and relief because He has already finished what He set out to do. As we continue to seek Him and what He has in store for us may we have moments of peace and rest in the work He has already done! - MO

God, please give me Your rest today. In Jesus name

Who can I give life to today?

What makes you laugh?

1.

2.

3.

4.

5.

Thoughts from Micah:

Glory in the Bible has many meanings depending on when it's used. The Scripture below refers to Glory from the Hebrew word kabowd, which also translates to "abundance."

"And the Lord said to Moses, 'I will do the very thing you have asked, because I am pleased with you and I know you by name.' Then Moses said, 'Now show me your glory.' And the Lord said, 'I will cause all my goodness to pass in front of you, and I will proclaim my name, the Lord, in your presence... When my glory passes by, I will put you in a cleft in the rock and cover you with my hand until I have passed by. Then I will remove my hand and you will see my back; but my face must not be seen.'" (Exodus 33:17-23 NIV)

Did you pick up on that? Moses asked God to, *"Show me your glory."* This was after Moses' experienced the burning bush, the ten plagues, the splitting of the Red Sea, God ascending on Mount Sinai, the tent meeting, and yet after all those experiences with God, Moses still wants more of Him. Moses wanted to see God face to face.

Too often we call on God for help or to ask Him to forgive us because of another one of our mistakes or mess ups. What if we started calling on God and asking Him to show us his Glory, His Splendor, His Majestic ways, His abundance?

"When Aaron and all the Israelites saw Moses, his face was radiant, and they were afraid to come near him." (Exodus 34:29 NIV)

After Moses came down from Mount Sinai, his face was shining. He had experienced the Lord's glory and abundance! Moses had spent time with the Lord and it was evident to all who saw him.

God, show me your glory and help me to shine with your goodness. In Jesus name.

Who can I give life to today?

DAY 34

What have I been blessed with?

1.
2.
3.
4.
5.

"Love one another the way I loved you. This is the very best way to love. Put your life on the line for your friends." (John 15:13 MSG)

What can we do when life feels big and overwhelming? Give life to someone else! Make them feel like we are in this *together*. If left on our own for too long, it's far too easy to close ourselves off from others. One of the best solutions to fight melancholy is to give to someone who is struggling or help someone around us.

"We can all agree that we live in a world where it's often hard to see love in action. I don't want to dwell on the problems of the world. The news, social media, and society do a good enough job of displaying corruption and hate. I'd rather focus on what is GOOD and suggest solutions." - MO

"Put your life on the line for your friends." This verse always stumps me, I am sure it has a deeper meaning, however the simple version is: to get out of my own thoughts of anxiety, sadness, disappointment, unknowns, confusion, loss....And give life to someone else.

What are practical ways to do this?

- Send a message to someone telling them how great they are!
- Surprise a friend with something small! (Example: a few weeks ago my son's friend unexpectedly dropped of Chick-fil-A milkshakes at our door)
- Write a note. (Or five notes!)
- Give a compliment! (Your words are powerful! One compliment can change someone's whole day.)

Who can I reach out to today?

God, show me who needs my encouragement. I give You what I am struggling with _____. Help me to choose You and Your loving thoughts about me, even when I can't figure out what tomorrow is going to look like. Give me the courage to reach out to others and show them your love. In Jesus name

Who can I give life to today?

DAY 35

I'm grateful for:

1.
2.
3.
4.
5.

"My counsel is this: Live freely, animated and motivated by God's Spirit. Then you won't feed the compulsions of selfishness. For there is a root of sinful self-interest in us that is at odds with a free spirit, just as the free spirit is incompatible with selfishness...so that you cannot live at times one way and at times another way according to how you feel on any given day. Why don't you choose to be led by the Spirit?"(Galatians 5:16-18 MSG)

Have you realized in this season that we are in that on any given day our emotions can be all over the place? Our emotions surrounding all of the life changes that have happened can feel like riding a roller coaster, but we don't have to let our feelings tell us what to do. Instead we can invite God's Spirit to help us.

It's great to acknowledge a feeling and then give it to Him. Then we can do something GREAT!

For example: "God, I feel so disappointed about _____ . I miss _____. Please fill me with Your hope." Then go reach out to someone or go do something you love.

We are not stuck in whatever we are feeling, we can choose to let His Spirit lead us.

God, fill me with Your love, joy, and hope today. All day long remind me to choose thoughts wisely. Show me who to reach out to today. In Jesus name

Who can I give life to today?

DAY 36

I am thankful for:

1.
2.
3.
4.
5.

"My God will meet all your needs according to the riches of his glory in Christ Jesus." (Philippians 4:19 NIV)

Choose Life to the Fullest is about one day at a time. Choosing to focus on the good things every morning, day after day changes our perspective. Over time, this habit transforms us into a thankful person, who enjoys life and can give life to others.

I have been thinking about short-term workouts or diets, the ones with those eye-catching titles that drive us to want to change and improve. Once we start diving into these challenges, we realize their title means a life-style change. For instance, if you are a basketball player you may do a workout that promises you can improve your vertical jump if you do this workout for 30 days in a row. What is assumed but maybe not stated is if you stop after the thirty days, you might have improved for a short time, but not permanently.

Life to the fullest is not a 90 day program, it's a life-style! Every morning you can *choose* to:

1. Wake up and write five things you are thankful for.
2. Read a Bible verse and ask yourself how it applies to your life.
3. Say a prayer inviting Jesus in, to all your life stuff...good and hard.

I do this every morning, because it makes me better. I don't enjoy myself when I'm focused on all the negatives, and I forget to prioritize my relationship with Jesus. Life feels heavy and hard unless I invite Him in.

Jesus, I want the life-style of thinking thankful, growing in my faith, and inviting You into everything. Show me how to grow in this. In Your name

Who can I give life to today?

What is good in my life?

1.

2.

3.

4.

5.

Thoughts from Micah:

"As Jesus was walking beside the Sea of Galilee, he saw two brothers, Simon called Peter and his brother Andrew. They were casting a net into the lake, for they were fishermen. 'Come, follow me, Jesus said, 'and I will send you out to fish for people.' At once they left their nets and followed him." *(Matthew 4:18-20 NIV)*

Peter and his brother, Andrew, weren't looking for Jesus. But Jesus was looking for Peter and Andrew. Think about that...the Savior of the world was looking for these two brothers while they were simply going about their day. Jesus *pursued* them. Picture it, Peter and Andrew just casting nets fishing and this guy (Jesus) shows up and invites them to come hang out with him.

Put yourself in their position. Maybe you're at school, practice, or home, minding your own business eating dinner, doing homework, or in the middle of a game or match. The same Savior that showed up to Peter and Andrew, is inviting you to follow Him! He asks you, will you come with me? Jesus didn't just command, He invited! He pursues us just as He pursued them.

If I'm being honest, sometimes it's easy to read the stories in the bible and think, "Well duh! Of course I would have gotten up and followed Jesus." But we have that same opportunity every single day. It can be difficult to imagine Jesus coming to me and asking me to follow Him. I've struggled to understand why Jesus would want me. He knows everything about me...even the bad and ugly. Would he really come to me and invite me to follow him? To hang out with him? To do life with Him?

This story about Jesus, Peter and Andrew leads me to believe that Jesus is so loving I can't fully comprehend why He would extend invitations to me. Time after time, mess up after mess up, failure after failure, sin after sin...our Father *still* invites me! He is inviting you too. All you have to do is accept his invitation. - MO

Jesus, I accept Your invitation and Your love and forgiveness. Thank you for pursuing me. I invite You into every area of my life.

Who can I give life to today?

DAY 38

What do I love?

1.
2.
3.
4.
5.

"Don't be afraid, I've redeemed you. I've called your name." *(Isaiah 43:1 MSG)*

God knows our name. He is always calling us to Himself, to relationship with Him, to draw close to His heart. He is constantly pursuing us with relentless love. We are dear to His heart. God embraces us everyday, not just on the days we feel like we have it together or are succeeding. He embraces us on our best day and on our worst. He embraces us regardless of what we do, because He loves us for who we are, His sons and daughters, His masterpiece, His treasure.

He knows our darkest thoughts and the longing in our heart. We can talk to Him. We can invite Him into our moments, our thoughts, our struggles, our unknowns, our fears, our extraordinary days and our ordinary ones. He understands and will walk through life with us. We can give Jesus our dreams, hopes, goals, mistakes, disappointment, longings and more. He will meet us in our need and we will find rest and peace.

What do you think God thinks when He thinks about you?

Do I think about God embracing me?

What am I holding onto that I need to give to God?

Jesus, thank You for knowing me, I invite You into my thoughts, my relationships, my hopes and dreams, my great days and my bad days. Show me more of Your heart for me. In Jesus name

Who can I give life to today?

DAY 39

What five things are good in my life?

1.
2.
3.
4.
5.

Life with God is an amazing adventure!

"My grace is enough; it's all you need. My strength comes into its own in your weakness. Once I heard that, I was glad to let it happen. I quit focusing on the handicap and began appreciating the gift. It was a case of Christ's strength moving in on my weakness. Now I take limitations in stride, and with good cheer, these limitations that cut me down to size— abuse, accidents, opposition, bad breaks. I just let Christ take over! And so the weaker I get, the stronger I become." (1 Corinthians 12:8-10 MSG)

God woke me up with this verse. I like to read the Message version because of the clear everyday language it uses. In this passage Paul is talking about his weakness, and how he is actually thankful for it, because it caused him to focus on God's grace and strength.

We can ask ourselves:

- What is my weakness or limitation?
- How can I invite God and His power into this weakness?

Most of us are very aware of our weaknesses. God doesn't want us to try to hide our struggles from Him, He wants us to invite Him into them! We can be like Paul and, *"Let Christ take over!"*

Jesus, I invite You into my weaknesses, thank You for wanting to be in my moments with me. Thank You that Your grace covers my shame and guilt and allows me to accept forgiveness and live in Your strength, relying on You. In Your name

Who can I give life to today?

What is good in my life?

1.
2.
3.
4.
5.

"If you loved me, you would be glad that I'm on my way to the Father because the Father is the goal and purpose of my life." (John 14:28 MSG)

Thoughts from Micah:

Believe it or not, we create routines without even knowing it. If you're a basketball player you might start to do the same things before you shoot every free throw. If you're a tennis player you might bounce the ball the same amount of times before you toss it up to make the serve. If you're a baseball player then you start doing the same thing as you get in the box. If you are in a band or involved in theater you might have a go-to warm-up or a certain kind of tea you have to drink before a show.

Why do we do this? There is a certain level of comfort in repeating the same thing while in the process of competing. It's part of the preparation. It's having a familiarity of doing what's known or comfortable prior to the outcome of the unknown—after you take the shot, make the serve, swing the bat, or step on stage.

As my career progressed I began to be more intentional about establishing my routine. A few things involved in my routine were: pre-game preparation, dieting, training regimen between games during the offseason, rest and recovery, and post game journaling—after both the good and poor outings.

We know that Jesus regularly spent alone time with the Father in prayer and communication. Perhaps Jesus went to the Father because it was His comfort place and In this place He was known. Perhaps Jesus knew it would help prepare Him for the battle and unknowns ahead. - MO

What are your routines in your sport or hobby?

In your spiritual life?

God, help me to establish routines that will grow me in my faith and in the things I love. In Jesus name

Who can I give life to today?

DAY 41

What am I thankful for?

1.
2.
3.
4.
5.

"Don't fret or worry. Instead of worrying, pray." (Philippians 4:6 MSG)

How do we ask God? With how quick the days and weeks can go by, it's often hard to slow down and talk to God. It can be difficult to figure out what we should be thanking God for and what we should be asking him for. Asking requires slowing down. Asking requires vulnerability.

Some of us resist this because it requires letting go and entrusting what we are asking for fully to God's plans. Asking God for things is wrapped up in what we think about God and what we think about life. God's heart for us is good, He wants life to be full for us.

One way I do this is to write down my prayer needs and the things I worry or stress about. Sometimes, I don't even realize what I was worried about until I stop and write. This only takes about five minutes.

What do I think about constantly?

What am I trying to figure out and need God's help with?

What gets me down that I need to give to God?

These are the things we can pray about.

Jesus, I invite You into my day, my thoughts, and my stresses. I give You everything. Please take my feelings of stress and worry away. In Your name

Who can I give life to today?

What are five things in life I enjoy?

1.
2.
3.
4.
5.

"As iron sharpens iron, so a friend sharpens a friend." *(Proverbs 27:17 NLT)*

Thoughts from Micah:

When you think of a true friend what do you think? Better yet, *who* do you think of?

"The definition of a true friend is someone who has your back, no matter what. They watch out for you and ensure you are not in danger. They will never purposely lead you into making decisions that aren't good for you. A true friend will always have your best interest at heart." (Smykowski, 2021)

One of my all time favorite verses is Proverbs 27:17. After reading this I ask you, are the people you are surrounding yourself with true friends? Are they there for you? Are your friends holding you accountable for your choices and actions? Are they "sharpening" you and encouraging you to be better?

It's important to identify where you want to go in life and who you want to be, and surround yourself with friends who will help—not drag you down or hold you back—you get there! It's also good for you to try to be that person in *your* friend's lives! Be the kind of friend to others you want for yourself! - MO

Jesus, I invite you into everything in my life. Send me friends that will bring me closer to you and the life you have for me. Help me to be that friend to others. In Your name

Who can I give life to today?

DAY 43

What are five good things in my life?

1.
2.
3.
4.
5.

Thoughts from Micah:

Fix your eyes on Jesus. Give him everything, everyone, and all of you.

"Let us throw off everything that hinders and the sin that so easily entangles. And let us run with perseverance the race marked out for us, fixing our eyes on Jesus, the pioneer and perfecter of faith. For the joy set before him he endured the cross, scorning its shame, and sat down at the right hand of the throne of God. Consider him who endured such opposition from sinners, so that you will not grow weary and lose heart." (Hebrews 12:1-3 NIV)

Fix your eyes on Jesus so that you can run the race marked out for you. I personally don't believe we are able to come to a place of surrender without keeping our eyes on Jesus. Here we are talking about surrendering *everything* (not just the easy things) and relying on God! As I write this, I'm reminded it's a constant reliance (daily, hourly, minute by minute, moment by moment, situation by situation) and not just a one time thing.

Peter walked on water. Let me say that again...Peter *walked* on water. He was an ordinary man, just like us, and yet he did the impossible! But as soon as he took his eyes off Jesus, his faith wavered and he began to sink. He let his surroundings and fear get to him instead of trusting that God had a path and a plan right in front of him.

Fix your eyes on Jesus. Refuse to look at anyone or anything else. Turn your eyes away from your circumstances, your limitations, your fears, and your worries. Stay focused on Jesus. He will never fail you. He is a good Father.

Jesus, I give you everyone and everything and me. I am fixing my eyes on You, Show me what "walking on water" looks like in my life. In Jesus name

Who can I give life to today?

What am I enjoying?

1.
2.
3.
4.
5.

"The righteousness of God has been made known, to which the Law and the Prophets testify. This righteousness is given through faith in Jesus Christ to all who believe. There is no difference between Jew and Gentile, for all have sinned and fall short of the glory of God, and all are justified freely by his grace through the redemption that came by Christ Jesus." (Romans 3:21-24 NIV)

Thoughts from Micah:

Becca and I were chatting about the power of focusing on one word. During different times in my career and life I have picked a word to focus on. My rookie year, my word was "grace." I felt an overwhelming draw to the word and what it means. As Jesus followers, grace means, "The free and unmerited favor of God."

Grace was an easy word for me to choose back in 2007 when I made the 25 man roster for the DBacks Big League team. I knew God's favor was in the midst of it all.

I took the word grace and applied it to my career and life at that moment. I remember during that season it was part of my password for different logins, posted in my locker, and written under the bill of my hat. For me, I needed to see this word everywhere as a reminder of God's favor. The grace God showed us by sending Jesus to the cross to die for us is the ultimate meaning of the word!

Do you have a positive word in mind? (Ex: grace, faith, trust, risk, give) If not, ask the Holy Spirit to provide you one. Consider writing it on your hand or on a sticky note and placing it on your mirror, nightstand or phone in the coming days, weeks, and months so you can look down and refer to it to help reposition your thinking and perspective! - MO

Jesus, I invite you into every aspect of my life. Give me a word that will motivate me to Think great. In Your name

Who can I give life to today?

DAY 45

What is good in my life?

1.
2.
3.
4.
5.

"I have loved you with an everlasting love, I have drawn you with loving-kindness." (Jeremiah 31:3 NIV)

What would your best friend say to you if they knew what you were really thinking or struggling with?

How would they encourage you during this season?

Friends are usually kinder to us than we are to ourselves. We can tell ourselves the same messages a great friend would tell us. Or we can focus on our negatives and continually remind ourselves of those things we just don't like about us. Focusing on our weaknesses or failures is not motivating and it has a negative effect.

A great friend would encourage us saying, "You are doing a great job." "Keep going!" Thinking great leads to living great!

What messages are you giving yourself?

Are these thoughts life-giving?

God, help me to stop when I want to focus on the negative. Remind me what You say about me. In Jesus name

Who can I give life to today?

What is good in my life?

1.
2.
3.
4.
5.

"The boat was far out to sea when the wind came up against them and they were battered by the waves. At about four in the morning, Jesus came toward them walking on the water. They were scared out of their wits. 'A ghost!' they said, crying out in terror. But Jesus was quick to comfort them. 'Courage, it's me. Don't be afraid.' Peter, suddenly bold, said, 'Master, if it's really you, call me to come to you on the water.' He said, 'Come ahead. Jumping out of the boat, Peter walked on the water to Jesus. But when he looked down at the waves churning beneath his feet, he lost his nerve and started to sink. He cried, 'Master, save me!' Jesus didn't hesitate. He reached down and grabbed his hand. Then he said, 'Faint-heart, what got into you?' The two of them climbed into the boat, and the wind died down." (Matthew 14:24-33 MSG)

I have been thinking about this passage since Micah wrote about it a few days ago.

Peter saw Jesus walking on the rough waves and had enough courage to go to Him, but something made Peter take his eyes off Jesus. Something made Peter start to sink. Did he start focusing on his own strengths, instead of looking to God's? Did Peter realize He was doing the impossible and become afraid? Did Peter start focusing on the waves around him, instead of the constant presence of Jesus? What happened?

What happens in our own life when everything is going well but then we start falling?

When Peter called for him, Jesus *immediately* reached down to help Peter. I love that! We can always call out to Jesus.

Do I call out to Jesus when I start falling (mentally, emotionally, or even in my life stuff-school, sports, relationships, etc.)? Why or why not?

Jesus, I want to stay focused on You. Help my thoughts to stay on You when I am walking through unknowns or when I am doing something courageous. In Your name

Who can I give life to today?

What am I grateful for?

1.
2.
3.
4.
5.

"Jesus Christ is the same yesterday, today, and forever." (Hebrews 13:8 NIV)

"Grateful is a feeling, gratitude is a choice." - Reed Moore

Choosing gratitude continually, moment by moment, day after day leads us to enjoy our life! Our feelings follow this choice.

We can repeatedly choose to be grateful for the things in our life, the people around us, our home, our school or work, our health, our sport hobby, friendships, God's heart for us, the little things we enjoy, there is so much to be grateful for!

If we live as if each moment is a gift, we give our best in every area of life in those moments.

If we repeatedly thank God all day long for the little things, we walk around grateful. When we are grateful we enjoy life, which leads to life to the FULL for us. Also, living grateful helps us give life to the FULL to others around us.

Every moment we get to choose.

Jesus, I am grateful for _____, empower me to choose to think thoughts of gratitude throughout the day. I give You everything and everyone and I give You me. In Your name

Who can I give life to today?

DAY 48

What is good in my life?

1.
2.
3.
4.
5.

"The Lord replied, 'My Presence will go with you, and I will give you rest.'" (Exodus 33:14-18 NIV)

People let us down, even those close to us. Yet, once we decide to put our trust in Jesus and invite Him into our life, He promises to never leave us. When we choose Jesus and He gives us His Spirit we have a friend with us at all times!

"I'm telling you these things while I'm still living with you. The Friend, the Holy Spirit whom the Father will send at my request, will make everything plain to you. He will remind you of all the things I have told you. I'm leaving you well and whole. That's my parting gift to you. Peace. I don't leave you the way you're used to being left—feeling abandoned, bereft. So don't be upset. Don't be distraught." (John 14:25-27 MSG)

The Holy Spirit is part of God and He lives with us to remind us of God's truth and love. Even though I grew up in church, this concept can be so complicated, so this is how my brain can simplify it. The Holy Spirit speaks the truth of Jesus and reminds me to stay on track. The Holy Spirit is the part of Jesus that lives in my heart.

Knowing that the Spirit of God is always with me gives me great peace. If you gave your life to Jesus in a prayer, then His Spirit is always there to help, guide, and befriend you.

What does it mean that God's presence is with us?

Do I feel alone? When?

In what ways can I remind myself the Holy Spirit is always with me and will never leave me?

We are never alone. The Presence of God is with us always.

Jesus, I invite You into my day, my moments, my school and work, and all of my thoughts. May Your Spirit guide my choices. In Your name

Who can I give life to today?

What is good in my life?

1.
2.
3.
4.
5.

"'For I know the plans I have for you,' declares the Lord, 'plans to prosper you and not to harm you, plans to give you hope and a future.'" (Jeremiah 29:11 NIV)

Did you know that we act out and live our lives based on what we think? Did you know the enemy knows the battle going on in you? Fear, worry, temptation, feelings of lack of worth or value, uncertainty...

Oftentimes you can see where you want to be, but just don't know how or, even *if*, you'll get there. During these times we can feel stuck. If you have ever felt this way, I can relate. There are things that you can do to help you get to where you want to be! Or even better, where you believe God wants you to be and His plan for you, because His plan is the BEST!

Remember today, if you are experiencing any of the above or feel the world is upon you, just by speaking Jesus' name out loud (under your breath or as loud as you can), a supernatural peace overcomes your innermost being! I encourage you to try it and maybe recite the powerful Name of JESUS over and over a few times!

What am I "living out?"

Jesus, I invite You into my thoughts and life, rescue me from the enemy, in Your name.

Who can I give life to today?

DAY 50

What am I excited about?

1.
2.
3.
4.
5.

"The Lord, himself, goes before you and will be there with you. He will never leave you nor forsake you. Do not be afraid; do not be discouraged." *(Deuteronomy 31:8 NIV)*

Thoughts from Micah:

The other day I read this quote by Jim Rohn, "You cannot change your destination overnight, but you can change your direction overnight."

What does this mean in your life?

I believe it starts with choosing! Becca has been writing about this for a long time now. Too often we try to change our destination (our end goals) but don't change our direction (what we are doing with each moment we are given right now). It might be trying to make the team, earning that scholarship, achieving straight A's, or getting that girl or guy to like us. Those are all great and good solid destinations to want to land, but if you don't start taking the right steps now, you'll never get there. If you don't start practicing, you probably won't make the team. If you don't apply yourself to getting scholarships or good grades, they might slip through the cracks. If you don't start being the person who *you* would want to be with, why would the person you want to date want to be with you? It's often a process. Look ahead to where you want to end up, and start taking steps to get you there.

I believe God gives us the desires of our heart and I believe he wants us to reach the destinations we so desperately desire. Go for it! May God lead, guide, and help you in your pursuit to the end goals!

Jesus, I invite You into my thoughts and my life. Show me each step to take as I choose the direction You have for me. In Jesus name

Who can I give life to today?

What is great in my life?

1.
2.
3.
4.
5.

"But the fruit of the Spirit is love, joy, peace, forbearance, kindness, goodness, faithfulness, gentleness and self-control. Against such things there is no law." (Galatians 5:22 NIV)

You don't have to wait for a new year or a new month to start a new goal. It's okay to keep it simple sometimes.

Think about one word you want to embrace- a word that will motivate you to grow, or a lens or filter to think through. For three years, my word was peace. It took three years because learning to be peaceful was a long journey for me. It's okay if it takes you a while to lean into your word. Other ideas could be any of the Fruits of the Spirits from today's verse.

I picked a new word at the beginning of August. Entrust. When I picked this word, I didn't realize that God would ask me to entrust so much into His care. Putting this word into practice means that I'm constantly reminded to give Him my unknowns, my stresses, my anxiety or frustrations.

What is your word?

How have you been challenged to put this word into practice?

Write this word in places where it will remind you to live it. Invite God to help you in this word.

Jesus, I want to be _____ (motivated, giving, confident, joyful, peaceful, fearless, courageous, kind). Help me to be more like You. I invite You to help me. In Jesus name

Who can I give life to today?

What five things am I thankful for?

1.
2.
3.
4.
5.

Words and thoughts from Micah:

"Ask and it will be given to you; seek and you will find; knock and the door will be open." (Matthew 7:7 NIV)

This verse isn't about blind faith. It's about being obedient to God and listening to Him. Our part is to ask, seek, knock, but God is the one who will give, find, and answer.

Our responsibilities are simple. Too often we try to play God's role. What are you asking for, seeking out, or knocking on? Go before God and ask boldly, but be patient and let God do what only he can do.

What does "ask, seek, knock" look like for me today in my walk with God?

Jesus, I invite You into what I'm asking for, the desires in my heart. I want to know You more and understand Your great love for me, I give You me. Thank you for every good thing in my life. In Your name

Who can I give life to today?

Five things that make me smile:

1.
2.
3.
4.
5.

"This is what I want you to do: Ask the Father for whatever is in keeping with the things I've revealed to you. Ask in my name, according to my will, and he'll most certainly give it to you. Your joy will be a river overflowing its banks!" (John 16:23-24 MSG)

"I got this."

How many of us have said that?

Yesterday, Micah talked about our responsibility to ask God. Asking requires a shift in our thinking from, "I got this," to, "I give You this." Have you ever been around a two or three-year old and tried to help them?" I can do this by myself!" is often their response. I can see myself in that response.

God encourages us to give Him everything: our needs, our worries, our unknowns, our dreams and longings, our sadness, our struggle, our friendships, and our negative thoughts. If I don't slow down and realize my stubbornness and my need for Him. In essence, I am saying, "I got this, I don't need you."

If we know the heart of God, we won't mind asking Him for help. His heart is overflowing with love for us. If God had DNA it would be love. Asking means trusting His heart and Who He is.

If I could have an audible conversation with God, what would I ask Him?

What keeps me from talking to God about this now?

Do I believe God's heart for me is love? Why or why not?

God, I want to believe Your heart for me is good even when life doesn't always feel good. I ask You to help me with _____ . I invite You to show me Your love and Your heart for me. In Jesus name

Who can I give life to today?

DAY 54

What is good in my life?

1.
2.
3.
4.
5.

"Dear children, let's not merely say that we love each other; let us show the truth by our actions." (1 John 3:18 NLT)

Words and thoughts Micah:

Ask, Seek, Knock." (Matthew 7:7). Recently we talked about asking for God's help and letting Him in. Today let's focus on the knocking part. While I believe asking and seeking are equally important, and take action on our part, knocking involves physical movement.

Think about it, when you go up to your neighbors house and knock on the door, or when you are staying in a hotel with your team and you go down the hall and knock on their hotel room door, or when you're in college and knock on your friend's dorm room, it requires action. And it requires a response from whoever is on the other side. Sometimes we have to knock, and knock, and knock until someone finally hears and opens the door.

The majority of the time when someone opens the door, what's their response? It might be, "Hey, what's up you?" or they could say, "What can I do for you?" maybe even, "Come on in!"

We (Becca and I) believe that our Father is at the door before we walk up to it, before we raise our arm to begin the motion to knock, His hand is on the door handle turning the knob at our first strike. Our Father is waiting for us, ready to welcome us in!

Jesus, I invite you into my life. I'm so grateful that You choose to pursue a relationship with me. Show me how to live life with You day by day. In Your name

Who can I give life to today?

DAY 55

Five things I am thankful for:

1.
2.
3.
4.
5.

Thoughts from Micah:

Yesterday we read out of Matthew 7 about how we take the initiative to knock on our Heavenly Father's door. Today we are going to look at a passage in Revelation where Jesus knocks on *our* door.

"Look at me. I stand at the door. I knock. If you hear me call and open the door, I'll come right in and sit down to supper with you. Conquerors will sit alongside me at the head table, just as I, having conquered, took the place of honor at the side of my Father. That's my gift to the conquerors!"(Revelation 3:20-21 MSG)

When you read that verse, what is the Holy Spirit saying to you? What I hear is that our God is pursuing us and if we hear Him and open the door, He's coming on in! By Him knocking on our door, He wants to build a relationship with us. He wants to hang with me and you. Not only does it say that He knocks, Jesus says "I'll come *right in* and sit down to supper with you." I don't know about you or your household, but I can't recall a time in my lifetime when any strangers came in and sat down to have supper.

Friends do that, people who we want to have a relationship with. Inviting someone into your kitchen and home is like calling someone family. Is that what you want? To call Jesus family? I do! Could you imagine the Savior Himself knocking on your door and asking to come in to hang and have a meal? Hopefully we got steak, mac and cheese, and one of Nonni's pound cakes on the menu.

Jesus, I invite you into every area of our life. Come on in!

Who can I give life to today?

Five good things in my life:

1.
2.
3.
4.
5.

"Don't copy the behavior and customs of this world, but let God transform you into a new person by changing the way you think. Then you will learn to know God's will for you, which is good and pleasing and perfect." (Romans 12:2 NLT)

Don't fall into a trap of what society tells you to do or say. I love this verse, *"Let God transform you into a new person by changing the way you think."* Things swirl in our minds. Sometimes we don't even realize it. We think about the what ifs. We go through scenarios in our thoughts. Tomorrow's unknowns can bother us. But God can take these thoughts and transform them into His will. His good, pleasing, and perfect will.

"(God,) I give You everything and everyone." (Get Your Life Back John Eldredge)

As I am reading this book, the prayer above stood out to me. The author says he prays this everyday throughout the day. For the last two weeks, every time a swirl of thoughts enters my mind, I have been saying, "God, I give you everything and everyone." Doing this prayer has taken away my need to "figure it out" in my thoughts. God's heart for us is good, so good that He sent the Rescuer, Jesus. So we can trust Him with everything and everyone!

God led me to another element of this prayer, "I give You (God) me." Not just my life, but everything, even the parts of me I don't like. When regrets or life-situations bring me pain, I can give all of that to God. When we do this, we are immediately able to stop focusing on our weakness and focus on life going on around us and the needs of others.

I encourage you to try this for a month. Every time a swirl of negative thoughts about life, others, or yourself enters your mind, whisper this prayer to God: "God, I give You everything and everyone. God, I give You me. In Jesus name." Sometimes it can be helpful to make a list of the things you're worried about and pray each one to God.

Jesus, I invite You into every area of my life. I give You "everything and everyone." In Your name

Who can I give life to today?

DAY 57

Five great things in my life?

1.
2.
3.
4.
5.

"Jesus often withdrew to lonely places and prayed." (Luke 5:16 NIV)

Thoughts from Micah:

I was mowing the yard yesterday and these words came to me: pray, prepare, praise, repeat...

Today, let's focus on prayer. When we take a look at Jesus' life, He is constantly turning to God in prayer. He would often sneak away on His own to take time to connect with Him. In Matthew chapter 6, we are encouraged to spend alone time with the Father just like Jesus did. *"But when you pray, go into your room, close the door and pray to your Father."* (Matthew 6:6 NIV)

A little further down in the same chapter (Matthew 6:9-14), Jesus teaches us how to pray with the Lord's Prayer. Six things we can draw from the Lord's Prayer:

1. Address God's rightful place as the Father.
2. Worship and praise God for who He is and all that He has done.
3. Acknowledge that it's God's will and plans are in His control and not our own.
4. Ask God for the things we need.
5. Confess our sins and repent (turn away from them, and choose a better path).
6. Request protection and help in overcoming sin and evil.

Jesus, I invite you into *everything* in my life. Thank you for your example on how to pray. In your name

Who can I give life to today?

DAY 58

I am thankful for:

1.
2.
3.
4.
5.

"All who seek the Lord shall find him and shall praise his name. Their hearts shall rejoice with everlasting joy." (Psalms 22:6 TLB)

"Way maker, miracle worker, promise keeper, light in the darkness, My God, that is who You are. You are here, touching every heart. I worship You." (Way Maker, Sinach)

What does it mean to worship God? We can worship God by the way we live—inviting Him into our everyday lives. We can worship Him by singing or listening to songs that praise His name. We can worship Him by using the gifts and talents he created in us. We can worship in all different ways.

At a time when my life was really hard, I learned the power of worship. I simply started telling God Who He is. Initially, I thought I was worshiping *for* God, because He desires our praises. A few days in, I realized worshiping Him reminded *me* how BIG He is and how much He cares for me. It reminded me that He *is* the Way Maker, Miracle Worker, Promise Keeper, Light in the darkness, My God.

Does anything keep me from worshiping God? Why?

What does praising God look like for me?

God, I praise You, Creator of all. Jesus I thank You for being the Savior and Rescuer of all. I ask Your Holy Spirit to fill my heart with an awareness of Who You are. In Jesus name

Who can I give life to today?

Five things I am thankful for:

1.
2.
3.
4.
5.

"Trust in the Lord with all your heart, and do not rely on your own understanding. Acknowledge him in all your ways, and he will make your paths straight." (Proverbs 3:5-6 NET)

The coffee mug I look forward to using every morning has "TRUST" written in big letters and the remainder of this verse. I know what it looks like to trust, but I got stuck on the word "acknowledge." What does it mean to acknowledge Him?

To acknowledge means, "To admit to be real or true; recognize the existence, truth, or fact of; to show or express recognition or realization of; to recognize the authority, validity, or claims of; to show or express appreciation or gratitude for; to take notice of or reply to." (dictionary.com)

Part of acknowledging God means to admit He is real, recognize His authority, appreciate Him, and reply to Him.

If I just thought about the first definition of acknowledge (to admit He is real), what would this mean for me?

God is real, He is love, He is the Creator, He cares about me, He made me, He knows me and loves me. How does knowing this change my thoughts about life and myself?

Further down the definition of "acknowledge" is, "To show or express appreciation or gratitude for:" This means that part of acknowledging God means thanking Him.

What can I thank God for?

Even when life is hard, there is always something we can be thankful for. God gave us salvation through the life, death, and resurrection of Jesus. We can thank God for this. Because of Jesus we can live free, we don't have to live in shame or guilt.

God, I know that You are God. You love me and You sent Your Son to rescue me. I want to recognize You throughout my day, everyday. I invite You into every area of my life. Remind me of the things I am thankful for when my thoughts go negative. In Your name

Who can I give life to today?

What is good in my life?

1.
2.
3.
4.
5.

Thoughts from Micah:

Yesterday Becca talked about this verse: *"Trust in the Lord with all your heart, and do not rely on your own understanding. Acknowledge him in all your ways, and he will make your paths straight." (Proverbs 3:5-6 NET)*

This verse has carried me through many highs and lows. August 18, 2007 became an impactful day to me because it was arguably the best all around performance in a game I've ever personally had, and it was my first big league game back home in Atlanta against the Braves.

More important than game day was the night before. I have never been one to get nervous or anxious about games, but this one was different. The night before I was wrestling with my inner thoughts and couldn't sleep. I texted a teammate, who was a veteran player and mentor of mine, and shared with him how I was struggling. His response was brief, but he closed with Proverbs 3:5-6. I read and read and read over this passage until an overwhelming peace came over me. To this day I acknowledge God in those moments preparing for, during, and after each game. I acknowledge how great our God is! - MO

What do I need to trust God with?

How can I acknowledge Him in these things?

Jesus, I invite you into every area of my life! I know that You are good and deserving of my trust. Give me courage and wisdom and guide my path. In your name

Who can I give life to today?

DAY 61

What is good in my life?

1.
2.
3.
4.
5.

"Each person is tempted when they are dragged away by their own evil desire and enticed." (James 1:14 NIV)

It's easier to do the right thing when life is good. Yet when life gets hard, making wise choices is more difficult. We can feel tired, weak, overwhelmed, or just annoyed. When we think and feel this way, we have a choice to run to God, or from Him.

We all need God. He is the Creator of all and designed us to live life with Him. We don't have what it takes to always choose the right thing by ourselves. As Christ followers, we need Jesus leading us and showing us where to go. When we are thinking negatively and our feelings start to follow, this is a time to be on high alert, this is a time when we can be tempted or enticed by the things we struggle with.

What do I do when I am thinking negative or feeling down?

Does this help me? Is this the best thing for me?

It's a red flag when our thoughts get negative or we feel like giving up. As soon as we notice this, we can say in our brain, "STOP!" and instead offer a prayer to God saying, "I invite You into this thought, my negativity, my choices, please help me and give me Your hope."

Who can I give life to today?

DAY 62

What is great in my life?

1.
2.
3.
4.
5.

"Your word is a lamp to guide my feet and a light for my path." (Psalms 119:105 NLT)

Words from Micah:

Have you ever felt the urge to sit down and read the Bible, but you're not sure where to start or what to read? I have, and still do sometimes. One of the most fascinating things about the Bible is that we can pick it up, thumb through the pages, land somewhere, and God speaks to us through the Holy Spirit!

As you prepare to open your bible, I encourage you to ask the Holy Spirit to speak to you as you read. Our Father, God almighty, hears us and speaks to us through His Living Word!

Just think about it, how many times have you read something and felt like *wham*...that applies to exactly what I'm dealing with or going through! This can be at random when you're searching what to read, or when you are doing a specific bible study and the reading for that day is so applicable, or it can come from another believer who shares a passage with you. Oftentimes God uses the people in our life, and speaks through them. Be open minded, listen, seek, and God will speak to you. He will show you. He will guide you. What you and I have to keep doing (no matter what) is reading His Living Word, believing, and listening to what He desires to share with us!

Jesus, I invite You into my thoughts, my moments, my day.

Who can I give life to today?

What is good in my life?

1.
2.
3.
4.
5.

"For You formed my innermost parts; You knit me [together] in my mother's womb. I will give thanks and praise to You, for I am fearfully and wonderfully made; Wonderful are Your works, And my soul knows it very well. My frame was not hidden from You, When I was being formed in secret, And intricately and skillfully formed [as if embroidered with many colors] in the depths of the earth. Your eyes have seen my unformed substance; And in Your book were all written The days that were appointed for me, When as yet there was not one of them [even taking shape]." (Psalms 139:13-16 AMP)

Words from Micah:

For years I've turned to this Scripture—particularly on birthdays of family members or people I love and care about, or my own birthday. Every time I read it, I remain in awe of how God *formed* us in our mother's womb. God *knew* us before we were even born. Furthermore, He knew and wrote all the days of each one of our lives before we were even fully made. Wow!

May our Father enable us to embrace just a piece of how marvelous He is. May we give Him all the glory, and praise Him for Who He is and for the creations He has beautifully made. I celebrate each of you today and the body, mind, and soul God formed into your being. He is the Creator and Author of life.

Jesus, thank you for creating me in your image. Thank you for the specific gifts and talents you have given me. Show me how to use them to bring You Glory. In Jesus name

Who can I give life to today?

DAY 64

Five things that make me smile:

1.
2.
3.
4.
5.

"So be content with who you are, and don't put on airs. God's strong hand is on you; he'll promote you at the right time. Live carefree before God; he is most careful with you." (1 Peter 5:6-7 MSG)

Another version says, *"Cast all your anxieties on Him, for He cares for you." (NIV)*

We can break this verse down:

- Be content with who I am.
- Know that God's hand is on my life.
- He will promote me.
- Live carefree (because of your trust in God).
- He is careful with me, both strong and kind.

Living carefree is all about casting our anxieties and fears on Him. When you go fishing, you cast out your line, but then you reel it back in. God never tells us to take our anxieties back. He wants us to give Him ALL of our worries. "Cast all your anxiety on him because he cares for you." (1 Peter 5:7 NIV) We can entrust *all* of our stuff to Him.

What do I worry about?

How can I give this to God?

Do I believe God's hand is on my life?

Can I choose to trust God by casting all my anxieties on Him?

God, thank You that Your hand is on my life, remind me of that when I feel like I am not enough. I cast, give, let go of _____ and I give You all of these things. In Jesus name

Who can I give life to today?

What am I thankful for?

1.
2.
3.
4.
5.

What do I think seconds before a big moment (game, show, test, event)?

"Summing it all up, friends, I'd say you'll do best by filling your minds and meditating on things true, noble, reputable, authentic, compelling, gracious—the best, not the worst." (Philippians 4:8 MSG)

Words about thoughts from Micah:

Our thoughts often guide and lead to our outcome. The best way I can explain this is in baseball terminology. The majority of my life I've been involved in baseball one way or another: playing, coaching, scouting, or simply enjoying being a fan of the game and watching.

When I played and was batting, I'd get two strikes and think "Uh oh, I'm about to strike out." So many hitters will agree. If they don't, they probably aren't being honest. As a spectator, I can see when a player is in the box and beating themselves up because of this mindset, or those who are shaking it off and getting their head back in the game.

So what can you do in that moment when a negative thought creeps in and threatens to overcome you? I had to learn to take a step back, out of the box, and replace the negative thought with a positive and encouraging one. When I was able to switch gears in my mind, my results got drastically better!

No matter what sport you play or what you are involved in, you can develop the mental disciplines to enable you to switch from a negative thought into a positive thought! In the heat of battle, I began to recite Scripture. Two of my favorite verses I liked to say to myself during games are: Philippians 4:13 and 2 Timothy 1:7. - MO

What do I think in stressful moments? What positive phrases or thoughts can I think instead?

Jesus, I invite You into my thoughts, reveal to me the negative thoughts I think, and help me to replace each one with Your truth.

Who can I give life to today?

What is good in my life?

1.
2.
3.
4.
5.

"Nothing can get between us and God's love because of the way that Jesus our master has embraced us." (Romans 8:39 MSG)

Living close to the heart of God is not determined by what we do or don't do; however, sometimes it affects how we feel about God. When we are not living the way we know God would choose for us, we feel separated from Him. Sometimes, as Christians, we can feel like we have to get ourselves back on track before we can be in God's presence again, but God doesn't want us to wait till we get our act together, He wants to *help* us get our act together.

Shame and guilt are weapons of the enemy. Inviting Jesus into our struggle and asking Him to forgive our wrong choices leads to life change. And what spurs this life change is knowing we are treasured by the heart of God! He is for us even when we aren't for ourselves. He loves us even when we feel unlovable. No matter how old we are, we will always be His children. It's so powerful to jump in and find ourselves nestled in the heart of God, knowing we are loved, not because of what we do but because of who we are.

Remember who we are and Whose we are. We are God's children and He is for us.

God, I accept all the love You have for me through a relationship with Jesus Christ. Meet me where I am, I give You me. In Jesus name

Who can I give life to today?

DAY 67

What do I enjoy?

1.
2.
3.
4.
5.

"This is the day the Lord has made. We will rejoice and be glad in it."
(Psalm 118:24 NKJV)

Today is going to be a GREAT day!

Some mornings God wakes me up with this simple thought, "Today is going to be GREAT!" Regardless of my circumstances, I can choose to tell myself this. The way we live is a result of our thoughts. If we tell ourselves today is going to be great, greatness will happen. Negativity will try to whisper in our ear and change our course, yet we can silence this by focusing on the good and positive.

Greatness can be simple. Greatness can be encouraging or helping someone. When we bless someone else greatness happens, whether we realize it or not! Greatness can be going for a run outside or doing something to better yourself. Greatness can be a good grade on a test. Greatness can be simple progress in any area of our lives. Greatness can be that we are constantly reminded of the things we enjoy (our thankfuls).

What can I do to make today great?

The Good News Translation of this verse ends with, *"Let us be happy, let us celebrate."* If we live in a constant celebration, we enjoy life more and others around us get to see God's light. Regardless of the stress that is going on, let's think, "Today is going to be a GREAT day. Let's make today great for those around us."

Jesus, remind me throughout today that today is a great day! May I give greatness to others and thank You that You made today for me—a free and full life! In Your name

Who can I give life to today?

DAY 68

What am I thankful for today?

1.
2.
3.
4.
5.

"I (Jesus) have come that they may have life and have it to the FULL!"
(John 10:10 NIV)

One thought can change our life! A repetitive, great thought can crush all the negative thinking, change our feelings, and empower us to greatness. We can stop and ask ourselves what we spend our time thinking about. Are these thoughts helping me?

We live out our thoughts, but we have the power to change them. If you've been stuck in the negative rut for a long time, changing the course of your thoughts may feel impossible. Jesus wants to be invited into this process. He wants to do life with us and invites us to do life with Him. Our thoughts lead toward our best life or away from it.

What would He want us to think about?

Jesus wouldn't want us to criticize ourselves or others in our mind. He doesn't want us to walk around afraid, discouraged and sad. That's not living life to the *full*, and he has promised us that we can. That's the whole reason he came!

Every time we think a discouraging thought we can change it to a hopeful thought. We can remember that God has a plan for our lives, that He is good, and His love could never be earned or lost but is *always* there for us.

Jesus, I invite You into my thoughts. Change each negative thought into a hopeful one. In Jesus name

Who can I give life to today?

DAY 69

What five things am I thankful for?

1.
2.
3.
4.
5.

"The prudent see danger and take refuge, but the simple keep going and pay the penalty." (Proverbs 22:3 NIV)

Words from Micah:

A few years ago I heard a great message and took notes. One phrase I wrote down was, "Somebody knows how to get you from where you are to where you want to be." The funny thing is, I didn't include in my notes who was speaking that day, but it was still a memorable message to me. If you believe in Jesus and the Holy Spirit, you know *Who* was really speaking that day.

The truth is that God speaks to us in various ways and through countless people. He might use one of our parents or our pastor, maybe a sibling or small group leader, it could be a great friend or teammate, it might even be a stranger!

The important thing is to listen. I also encourage you to invite Him to speak to you through others, and be bold enough to ask Him to use you to speak to others too!

Jesus, I invite You to lead me in every area of my life. Bring people into my life that speak Your wisdom. In Your name

Who can I give life to today?

What are five things I'm thankful for?

1.
2.
3.
4.
5.

"And I will ask the Father, and He will give you another Helper (Comforter, Advocate, Intercessor—Counselor, Strengthener, Standby), to be with you forever—the Spirit of Truth, whom the world cannot receive [and take to its heart] because it does not see Him or know Him, but you know Him because He (the Holy Spirit) remains with you continually and will be in you." (John 14:16-17 AMP)

Words from Micah:

Yesterday we discussed the different people in our life God could use to get a message across. Today let's talk about another person in our life God uses to speak to us. This "person" is called the Holy Spirit.

I grew up going to a few different churches, especially the older I got with baseball and traveling. Most of the churches I visited would speak about God the Father and Jesus the Son (the Savior); however, the Holy Spirit wasn't talked about a whole lot. As I've gotten older, I've studied more and believe strongly in the power of the Holy Spirit.

We accept Jesus into our heart and trust God to lead us, but we aren't done there. We also need to welcome the Holy Spirit into our lives on a regular basis. Before Jesus ascended into Heaven to sit at the right hand of God, He comforted His disciples. Jesus knew life would be tough, so He sent us a helper until He comes back for us. You and I can take great comfort in today's scripture and in the presence of the Holy Spirit! - MO

Jesus, I invite You to do life with me today and I invite the Holy Spirit into every area of my life. In Jesus name

Who can I give life to today?

DAY 71

What am I grateful for?

1.
2.
3.
4.
5.

Wherever we are in life and whatever stage we're at in our faith, we can always pray. Praying is simply talking to God. During difficult seasons or hardships it can feel a little difficult to pray, but talking to and relying on God does something amazing inside of us. It energizes us to keep going! We were made to connect with God. If we see God as someone Who loves us completely and knows us completely, nothing we say or think will ever surprise Him. Our conversations with God can be as comfortable as chatting with a best friend!

I found this one-liner prayer when I felt like I was at rock bottom and wanted to give up. I was desperate and needed a miracle. Although my prayer was not answered immediately, it still changed my life and worked miracles in the lives of those around me.

The one-liner goes like this, "I speak the resurrection power of Jesus over _____ (my life, my dreams, my relationship, this hurting person, what I struggle with and more)." This is what I pray when I want a miracle, this is what I pray when I am tired, this is what I pray when I am aware of how powerful God is.

The prayer came from this verse, *"If the Spirit of him who raised Jesus from the dead is living in you, he who raised Christ from the dead will also give life to your mortal bodies because of his Spirit who lives in you." (Romans 8:11 NIV)*

When we tell Jesus we believe in Him (His death and resurrection), give Him our life, and invite Him into our life, He gives us Himself and the same power that raised Jesus from the dead lives inside of us!

I encourage you to pray this powerful one-liner prayer, "I speak the resurrection power of Jesus over _____."

Who can I give life to today?

DAY 72

What five things am I thankful for?

1.
2.
3.
4.
5.

Words from Micah:

Jesus summarized all of Scripture with the first two commandments: *"Love the Lord your God with all your heart and with all your soul and with all your mind and with all your strength... Love your neighbor as yourself." (Mark 12:30-31 NIV)*

While loving God can be tough for us at times, it's understood why Jesus emphasizes this being the most important commandment. Let's talk about loving our neighbor, friends, and those around us. This can be more challenging for us than we realize. Think about the people in your life you love the most—your best friends, your family, your teammates. How often do you feel unloving toward them? Even our best friend can be difficult to love! How often do you feel unloved by others?

To love others well, we have to first understand how much God loves us. His love is one so big and vast you can't ever fully comprehend it. When we don't love ourselves—who God created in His own image—we can't love others fully. Have you ever heard the saying, "hurt people hurt people?" It's the same with people who don't feel loved themselves, they aren't that great at making others feel loved.

Let's take it a step further. Too often we view love as conditional; if they do this, buy me that, take me there, like the things I like, vote the way I vote, *then* they really love me. That's bad thinking and bad theology.

I believe Jesus wants us to focus on God's love first so we can understand how to love Him, how to love ourselves, and then how to love others. God's love is unconditional. God IS Love. Let me say that again...God's love is *unconditional*. There isn't a list of do's or don'ts for Him to love you, He loves you and wants what's best for you. May you seek His love and learn to love Him first, so He can enable you to love yourself and others unconditionally. - MO

Jesus, I invite You into everything in my life! Teach me how to love You first and show me ways I can love those around me. In your name

Who can I give life to today?

DAY 73

What is great in my life?

1.
2.
3.
4.
5.

"Every good present and every perfect gift comes from above, from the Father who made the sun, moon, and stars. The Father doesn't change like the shifting shadows produced by the sun and the moon." (James 1:17 GW)

What did you wake up thinking about? Did it motivate you? If not, you can choose to jumpstart your brain by thinking about five great things in your life. If you are struggling to find five thankfuls, scroll through photos on your phone. This always reminds me of fun memories I have with loved ones and gives me something to be thankful for.

There is a group of high school students I met a long time ago who changed the way I view life. In my counseling internship, I led a grief and loss group. Each of the students in the group had lost someone close to them. Once a week for two years we talked about the stages of grief and we walked through it together. This is what they taught me:

- Don't *ever* leave a conversation regretting what I said.
- Never forget to say, "I care," or, "I love you!"
- Don't let moments pass by. Treasure each one!
- Ask myself daily how I want to be remembered by those who are closest to me, and live that out.

Even though I was the counselor during these meetings, I was also the student. Taking in their thoughts, comments, regrets, hopes, and wishes changed how I leave conversations and helped shape my interactions with the ones I love.

What would it look like in your life to live every moment to the fullest?

What would it mean to leave every conversation without regret or harsh words?

What would it look like to live your life thinking about how you want to be remembered?

Jesus, I invite YOU into my moments. I invite You into my thoughts and feelings, which affect *everything*. Please shine through me by the way I treat others and live each day. Each moment is a gift from You. Thank You!

Who can I give life to today?

What is good in my life?

1.
2.
3.
4.
5.

"None of this fazes us because Jesus loves us. I'm absolutely convinced that nothing—nothing living or dead, angelic or demonic, today or tomorrow, high or low, thinkable or unthinkable—absolutely nothing can get between us and God's love because of the way that Jesus our Master has embraced us." (Romans 8:34 MSG)

When we wrap ourselves in the truth that we are loved by God, we can live life to the fullest. His love is enough to cover all of our sins, insecurities, and failures. He loves us completely. He loves us, because, to Him, we are all lovable. When this truth seeps down to the core of who we are it changes our self view. We start liking ourselves. Then we can give life to others.

"Love never fails (never fades out or becomes obsolete or comes to an end)." (1 Corinthians 13:8 AMPC)

Like most things in life, love is a choice. Choosing the way of love often means letting go of what we want. To figure out how to live love, we can ask ourselves, "In this situation or relationship, what does love look like?"

Love looks forgiving, love looks hopeful, love looks unselfish. Love gives, love encourages, love keeps going, love thinks the best, love gives what isn't deserved.

As we are in the season of thankfulness, may we accept God's love and give His love to the world around us.

What does giving love look like for me today?

God, I want to accept all the love You have for me through a relationship with Jesus. I invite You to fill my heart, mind, and life with Your love. Show me how to give Your love to others. In Your name

Who can I give life to today?

What five things are you thankful for this morning?

1.
2.
3.
4.
5.

"This resurrection life you received from God is not a timid, grave-tending life. It's adventurously expectant, greeting God with a childlike 'What's next, Papa?' God's Spirit touches our spirits and confirms who we really are. We know who he is, and we know who we are: Father and children. And we know we are going to get what's coming to us—an unbelievable inheritance! We go through exactly what Christ goes through. If we go through the hard times with him, then we're certainly going to go through the good times with him!" (Romans 8:15-17 MSG)

Living a life following Jesus is not boring or dull. In complete contrast, it's full of adventure! We can stress, worry, and fret...or we can live with a constant sense of anticipation asking, "What's next, God?" It may feel as if we are holding on to God's coattails as He leads us on what can feel like a roller coaster. But in reality, He is walking through our moments with us.

Many years ago, I realized Jesus was not way ahead of me expecting me to catch up to Him, or behind me counting my mistakes, but right beside me in my ups and downs. His love covers all of our sins, mistakes, wrong turns and wraps us in His grace and love. In that place He leads us while walking beside us on the amazing adventure He has for us.

What does this adventure require of us?

1. Accepting His forgiveness everyday. Shame and guilt are from the enemy, and we must not let them have any place in our lives.
2. Choosing to let His never-ending love cover _____ (our rejection, fear, anxieties, insecurities).
3. Ask God what He is leading us to and take a step, trusting in His plans for your life.

Obviously we don't know what tomorrow looks like in school, sports, work, ministry, friendships, etc. and that's okay! God does and He has great things in store for us. When we live in a constant mindset of adventure, we are more hopeful, more joyful, and we are better equipped to give life to others.

God, What do You have for me today? Lead me and show me Your great love for me. Help me to overflow with Your love and bring others closer to You through my example. In Jesus name

Who can I give life to today?

DAY 76

What five things am I grateful for?

1.
2.
3.
4.
5.

"Let us hold firmly to the faith we profess. For we do not have a high priest who is unable to empathize with our weaknesses, but we have one who has been tempted in every way, just as we are—yet he did not sin. Let us then approach God's throne of grace with confidence, so that we may receive mercy and find grace to help us in our time of need." (Hebrews 4:14-16 NIV)

Rejection. I hate it, don't you? Rejection hurts, it's like a punch to the stomach. If we choose to let rejection have power in our lives, it can stop us in our tracks and drive us to anxiety. It can steer our thoughts away from hope, steal a dream, make us feel unwanted or isolated—even when we are surrounded by people who love us.

Yesterday, I received a rejection email. For five years, I have been writing a book about choosing hope through hard times. The agent I sent it to emailed me back saying simply, "Your manuscript is not needed at this time."

What I wanted to do in that moment was give up. Stop taking risks, stop putting my writing out there, and just stay safe in my shell. Without risk there is no rejection, right? As I was chewing on these feelings, I texted my eighteen year old son, Owin, and told him what happened. This was his response, "Rejection is one step closer to success." The rejection still stung, but his encouragement was enough to pick back up and try again.

What can we do with rejection?

1. Face it. Own up to it.
2. Then give that pain to God and ask Him to give you peace, comfort and clear next steps.
3. Ask yourself what's motivating you to keep going. What's your "why?"
4. Keep your "why" in mind as you seek progress everyday. Keep going, work hard, and stay motivated!
5. Choose everyday to invite Jesus into everything.

Our thoughts about ourselves, our feeling of belonging and contentment, and our hope must come from Him; everything else leaves us empty, even when we reach our dreams.

Jesus, I give You the rejection I've faced. Take away the damage it has done in my heart and my thoughts. I choose to be hopeful! Walk beside me as I continue to risk, to walk in faith, to live the adventure that You have for me. In Jesus name

Who can I give life to today?

DAY 77

What are five things I'm thankful for?

1.
2.
3.
4.
5.

"Therefore, as we have opportunity, let us do good to all people, especially to those who belong to the family of believers." (Galatians 6:10 NIV)

Life-time friends are gifts from God. Those best friends who you don't have to see everyday, but you know that no amount of distance or time could wreck your friendship.

My life-time friend, Natalie Gibson, mentioned three things she tries to do everyday:

1. Compliment someone.
2. Encourage someone.
3. Have one meaningful conversation.

She went on to say, "I know it doesn't seem like much, but it might help in the world we live in now!"

What if we all did this in our school or work, at home or at church? When we choose to invite Jesus into everything, think the best about ourselves, and focus on the good things in our lives, we live out of an overflow of gratitude, which enables us to give to others.

I am going to join Natalie and try to do this everyday, and I encourage you to join us!

How can I encourage others today?

Jesus, fill me with Your love and remind me of the good things in my life, so that I live overflowing with Your kindness and give this to others. In Your name

Who can I give life to today?

What five things make me smile?

1.
2.
3.
4.
5.

"I know what I'm doing. I have it all planned out—plans to take care of you, not abandon you, plans to give you the future you hope for." (Jeremiah 29:11 MSG)

Words from Micah:

When I watched the first game of the 2020 World Series. A couple of thoughts rushed through my head before the game. First off, I was hoping it was my hometown team, the Braves, playing against Dusty Baker, my good friend and former manager's team, the Astros.

Another thought I had was wondering how many of the players in the game had dreamed their whole life of being there. I'll be the first to raise my hand, because I definitely dreamed of playing in the World Series and pitching in the opening game!

Your dream doesn't have to be the World Series, or even sports-related...it can be anything! Getting the lead role in a play, earning an academic scholarship, scoring that internship right out of college, or maybe you dream of going into politics and making positive change for our country. - MO

What has God planted in you to dream BIG and pursue with all your heart?

What steps are you taking every day to get there?

Often our dad used to tell me and my siblings, "Dream big and live large, because we have a big God." His words echo in my head often.

Jesus, I invite You into my dream. Show me how to live out the dreams that You have for me. In Your name

Who can I give life to today?

What five things am I grateful for?

1.
2.
3.
4.
5.

"God made the two great lights—the greater light (the sun) to rule the day, and the lesser light (the moon) to rule the night; He made the [galaxies of] stars also [that is, all the amazing wonders in the heavens]. God placed them in the expanse of the heavens to provide light upon the earth." (Genesis 1:16-17 AMP)

Words from Micah:

The news came on following the World Series game the other night. The reporter mentioned there was supposed to be a meteor shower that night and into the early morning hours. I thought, "hmm...I'm really tired but maybe I'll step outside and check it out before I go to bed."

While waiting, I found myself gazing into the midnight sky. For forty-five minutes I sat there marveling at God's masterpiece above. I felt so small! Here I was earlier in the night thinking about my dreams and doing big things, yet not an hour later I'm awestruck by God's imagination and creativity. The sky was crystal clear, lit up by the moon and stars. Frogs and crickets chirped in the woods. We live in a massive world, yet God is *all* knowing! God knows the number of stars in the sky, just how He knows the number of hairs on our head.

Jesus I invite you into everything in my life. I am amazed by Your creation.

Who can I give life to today?

DAY 80

Five things I'm grateful for:

1.
2.
3.
4.
5.

"He knows us far better than we know ourselves...That's why we can be sure that every detail in our lives of love for God is worked into something GOOD." (Romans 8:27-28 MSG)

A book I read in college was named, "Happiness is a Choice." I don't remember much of what the book said, but the title stuck in my mind, reminding me that I get to choose happiness every single day. Because happiness doesn't just happen, it's chosen. What we see, hear and think about determines what we focus on and where our path goes. Our focus determines our happiness.

If you were to go outside at night, you could probably hear cars passing by, crickets chirping, maybe voices from a neighboring house. If you focus on just one of the sounds, it becomes clearer, seemingly louder and the other sounds can disappear.

Our thoughts are like this too. We can choose which ones to focus on and put energy toward.

- We can focus on failures of yesterday or hope for today.
- We can focus on something negative said to us or something life-giving.
- We can focus on ourselves (our disappointments) or reach out to others.
- We can listen to the lies we tell ourselves or who God says we are.

Every detail He works into good, so we can choose hope and happiness.

Jesus, I choose happiness today. I give You all of the things in my mind that I focus on that steals that happiness. I invite You to live my moments with me.

Who can I give life to today?

DAY 81

What are five good things in my life?

1.
2.
3.
4.
5.

"For as he thinks in his heart, so is he." *(Proverbs 23:7 NKJV)*

Do you ever wake up and your mind is swirling? I do. Some mornings I wake up and my mind is full of trying to figure things out things. Simple things like schedules, and bigger things like next steps toward achieving a dream. In that moment, we have a choice: to stay in the swirl, or to give everything to God.

During my teenage years, I struggled with anxiety. My brain would stay in a swirl like this all day long. It wouldn't bother me until I realized that the people closest to me knew when my thoughts were swirling. It made me less patient, less peaceful, and no fun. I had to retrain my brain to choose to let the swirl of anxious thoughts go.

Retraining our brain is simple, but it takes a lot of repetition. When our brain starts worrying about all of the things (big and small). We can say, "God I give You _____ (name them one by one) in Jesus name." You can do this all day long if you need to.

When we do this we are choosing to let worry and anxiety go and trusting God with the process. Worrying and anxiety do not help get anything done.

God, I give You _____ in Jesus name.

Who can I give life to today?

Five things that make me smile:

1.
2.
3.
4.
5.

"I (God) have loved you with an everlasting love." (Jeremiah 31:3 NIV)

Years ago when I was on Young Life staff, I encountered Jesus in a new way. On a beautiful mountain in Colorado at Frontier Ranch, God whispered, "I love you, not because of what you do, but because of who you are. I, Jesus, absolutely love you."

I thought I already knew this, but if I was honest with God and myself, I held Him at a distance. I was so aware of His goodness and my failures. I couldn't embrace the fact that He wanted to be close to me, walk with me, live my moments with me, fill me with His all-consuming, unconditional, powerful, tender love. Trusting the love of Jesus was like jumping off the Colorado mountain I was sitting on into so many unknowns. I was forever changed by this conversation with God at Frontier Ranch.

If I stay in the reality of His great love, I like myself. If I don't, although His love never changes, I start focusing on my faults, failures, and past rejection. If I let His love fill my heart and my mind and what I think about me and others I live my life to the fullest!

The love of God shown through the life of Jesus is big enough to cover all of our sins, His love is big enough to handle all of our anxieties, His love is greater than our biggest fear, His love heals the deepest pain and memory, and His love transforms our mess into miracles.

Do I filter my thoughts about me through God's love?

How can I give my worries, failures and rejection to God?

Can I ask the love of God to become my identity (what I think about myself)?

Jesus, I invite You into my thoughts about me, You, and life. I accept the everlasting love that You have for me. In Your name

Who can I give life to today?

What is good in my life?

1.
2.
3.
4.
5.

"Those who think they can do it on their own end up obsessed with measuring their own moral muscle but never get around to exercising it in real life. Those who trust God's action in them find that God's Spirit in them—living and breathing God! Obsession with self in these matters is a dead end; attention to God leads us out into the open, into a spacious, free life. Focusing on the self is the opposite of focusing on God. Anyone completely absorbed in self ignores God, ends up thinking more about self than God...

But if God himself has taken up residence in your life, you can hardly be thinking more of yourself than of him. Anyone, of course, who has not welcomed this invisible but clearly present God, the Spirit of Christ, won't know what we're talking about. But for you who welcome him, in whom he dwells—even though you still experience all the limitations of sin—you yourself experience life on God's terms. It stands to reason, doesn't it, that if the alive-and-present God who raised Jesus from the dead moves into your life, he'll do the same thing in you that he did in Jesus, bringing you alive to himself?...With his Spirit living in you, your body will be as alive as Christ's!" (Romans 8:5-11 MSG)

Life to the fullest is not about ignoring the hard things, it's about choosing not to *focus* on them. If we ignore the hard things like rejection, pain, and sadness, it eventually catches up to us and can even stop us in our tracks or become a bigger problem. It's important to face the difficulties and take steps toward healing and growth if needed. We'll all go through difficult seasons—it's okay to feel frustrated, sad, or lonely. Choosing life to the fullest is just that, a choice, a choice to learn from the past and look forward to the future.

Sometimes, I wake up thinking about things that are hard, broken, or out of my control and I sense God calling me to pray about them and give it to Him instead of dwelling on all the bad. In that moment, I get to choose to trust God with all things.

Jesus I invite you into the good and the difficult. I give you everything (at home, work, school, in my relationships, dreams, sports, and finances). I give You me. In your name

Who can I give life to today?

DAY 84

I am grateful for:

1.
2.
3.
4.
5.

"The thief comes only to steal and kill and destroy; I have come that they may have life, and have it to the full." (John 10:10 NIV)

Recently, I dreamed that I was sitting in a crowd with hundreds of believers. The speaker stopped speaking to ask questions to the audience. The question was, "What is the enemy trying to steal from you? And what do you do about it?"

In my dream, as the speaker pointed to me, I immediately knew what to say. "The enemy is trying to steal my peace and make me afraid." I continued on by opening my hands and saying. "I entrust by praying this verse: (Inserting names and situations here) "_____ *I commit you to God [I deposit you in His charge, entrusting you to His protection and care]. And I commend you to the*

Word of His grace [to the commands and counsels and promises of His unmerited favor]. It's able to build you up and to give you [your rightful] inheritance among all God's set-apart ones (those consecrated, purified, and transformed of soul)." (Acts 20:32 AMPC)"

Life can feel out of control sometimes. When this happens, we can stop and ask ourselves, "What is the enemy trying to steal from me, and what do I do about it?"

Most mornings the enemy tries to steal my hope, joy, and happiness by reminding me of all the things that are out of control. My go to prayer is opening my hands and saying this verse, "I entrust (fill in the blank) into your protection and care."

Praying this daily changes me. We can live life to the full when you give things back to God. We can give Him anything that is sad or overwhelming, what we worry about, our fears, our hopes and dreams, and the people in our lives that we love.

God, I entrust _____ into Your care. In Jesus name

Who can I give life to today?

What am I thankful for?

1.
2.
3.
4.
5.

"Rejoice in the Lord always. I will say it again: Rejoice!" (Philippians 4:4 NIV)

Every day, we get 1,440 minutes. If we sleep for eight hours, it leaves 960 minutes each day.

We can ask ourselves:

- How am I living each minute?
- Am I living each moment to the fullest?
- In my day, do I give life to others?
- Do I choose to think thoughts that will help me enjoy life?

- Am I who I want to be each and every minute?
- If not, why?

We don't know how many minutes we will get in this life, so why not live each moment to the FULL!

A few times while writing these posts, I have referred to a group of high school teenagers that changed my life and my perspective. They were all part of a grief group and had lost someone dear to them. Each of them said the same thing, "If I just had one more moment with _____ (the person they lost)."

Each moment we can give life to someone else by our words, actions, and tone. When we give life to others, we enjoy life more. Each moment we can choose to live the best version of ourselves. How? By being thankful! By defining ourselves by God's great love and inviting Jesus to do life with us.

What are some moments I'm grateful for today?

God, I give You my moments, may I live life to the FULL. Jesus, I invite You into every area of my life. In Your name

Who can I give life to today?

What is good in my life?

1.
2.
3.
4.
5.

"For the Spirit God gave us does not make us timid, but gives us power, love and self-discipline." (2 Timothy 1:7 NIV)

Words from Micah:

Today's word is conviction. The particular usage of this word we are going to focus on is, "The quality of showing that one is firmly convinced of what one believes or says."

I'll never forget a conversation I had with my long time mentor, Cris Carpenter. Cris is an eight year Major League Baseball Pitcher and one of the most talented all around athletes I've ever known. It was my senior year in high school and we were preparing to make a run for our back-to-back state titles. Like we always did,

Cris and I were having a post bullpen conversation. During this particular one Cris said something really powerful, "MO, you have to be sold out, 100% *convicted* in what you're doing."

Right away something clicked for me, it didn't necessarily matter if the correct pitch was called by me or the catcher. What mattered the most is my conviction—my belief—in the pitch I was about to throw. Even before I went into my delivery, I had to be so convinced in my ability to make it, nothing else mattered.

As a fan, you can see this in certain players. As an opponent, it's that unspoken vibe you sense or see in the individual you are battling with. As a player, you know when you have it and it doesn't matter who is in the box or on the mound, because you have already beat them before you even release the ball. After being a scout and coaching for years, I learned a lot of times you can see the kids or players who remain confident and convicted in their approach, even in the heat of the battle. You also can see the ones who allow the moment to get the best of them and cave when they need to push through. - MO

Are you sold out and convicted in your abilities? What is keeping you from believing?

Ask a teammate, coach or friend who knows you well what they think.

God, help me to live out my convictions, and help me to live with purpose in every area of my life. In Jesus name

Who can I give life to today?

DAY 87

What is good in my life?

1.
2.
3.
4.
5.

Words from Micah:

Jesus answered, *"I am the way, and the truth, and the life. No one comes to the Father except through me."* (John 14:6 ESV)

This is what Jesus told His disciples when they were asking Jesus about Heaven. Jesus described earlier in verse two, *"I am going there (Heaven) to prepare a place for you."*

Have you ever wrestled with how God sent His Son, Jesus, to save YOU? Save the world, save others, save my friends and family, sure...but ME? If I'm being honest, I've struggled to understand how Jesus sacrificed Himself for ME.

Whether it's me or the enemy, there are things that stir up in me like: did you really ask Jesus into your heart when you were 10? Have you really believed in Jesus for the past 28 years? If so, why and how could you have possibly done this or that. How could you possibly have these kinds of thoughts? Do you *really* believe in Jesus and do you really trust in Him as your Savior. When there's an altar call or pastor inviting you to accept Him as your Savior, do you find yourself praying it (again)? Do you find yourself feeling prompted to raise your hand or stand (again) to profess your salvation (again)?

During these moments we can get frustrated, and think "Is my faith not strong enough?" Or, "Have I not believed enough in Jesus before now?" I'm no theologian...but I've had a relationship with Jesus for a long time, and in these moments of coming back to God I believe the Holy Spirit is calling on us. Even during the times we wrestle with our faith, God appoints the Counselor to speak to our hearts and comfort us, reminding us He's with us! *"The Counselor, the Holy Spirit, whom the Father will send in my (Jesus) name, will teach you all the things and will remind you of everything I have said to you." (John 14:26 NIV)* - MO

Jesus, I invite You to show me more of who You are and I invite You into every area of my life. In Your name

Who can I give life to today?

178

DAY 88

What five things am I thankful for?

1.
2.
3.
4.
5.

"But for you who welcome him, in whom he dwells—even though you still experience all the limitations of sin—you yourself experience life on God's terms. It stands to reason, doesn't it, that if the alive-and-present God who raised Jesus from the dead moves into your life, he'll do the same thing in you that he did in Jesus, bringing you alive to himself? When God lives and breathes in you (and he does, as surely as he did in Jesus), you are delivered from that dead life. With his Spirit living in you, your body will be as alive as Christ's!" (Romans 8:10-11 MSG)

Something wakes up inside of us when we invite Jesus into our life and heart. The emptiness is gone. The mystery of the Holy Spirit (which is a part of God) coming to live in us does something miraculous to our heart. His Spirit fills us with an identity in Him, He makes us alive by the Spirit He places in us. True life—life to the fullest—is found by welcoming Him into our daily activities and asking Him to walk each moment with us. By spending time with God each day, we are reminded of what we have inside of us—His love, joy, peace, goodness, kindness, and self-control.

If I have invited Jesus into my life, do I live in a realization that His Spirit is inside of me and always available to empower me and give me peace and courage each day?

Jesus, I invite You into my moments, my decisions, my thoughts, my heart, my sadness, my hopes, my relationships, my dreams, and my struggles. I want Your Spirit to do more than I can ask or imagine in my life. In Your name

Who can I give life to today?

DAY 89

What am I grateful for?

1.
2.
3.
4.
5.

"God is kind, but He is not soft. In kindness he takes us firmly by the hand and leads us into a radical life change." (Romans 2:4 MSG)

God is kind to us, He sees deep into our heart. In that place, He knows our rejection, our pain, our struggle, our hopes, our dreams, our desires. He loves us there in that place, even when we don't like ourselves. He is kind even though He knows us inside and out, because He loves us completely.

"He takes us firmly by the hand and leads us into radical life change." Because He knows this is where we will live life to the FULL. He guides and makes us face those things we struggle with such as: anger, insecurity, guilt and shame, fear, anxiety, failure, and resentment.

Is God leading me to face something?

He doesn't leave us stuck in the struggle, He leads us into radical life change, because He knows this is where real life is found and our best life will be lived.

God, in Your kindness, fill me in Your powerful tender love, please take me by the hand, lead me into the radical life change that You have for me. In Jesus name

Who can I give life to today?

Five good things in my life:

1.
2.
3.
4.
5.

"But if we hope for what we do not yet have, we wait for it patiently."
(Romans 8:25 NIV)

Some days it feels like we are riding on a roller coaster. We may start our day thinking about five great things (our thankfuls) and invite Jesus in and then...life happens.

Yesterday was like that for me. I started off my morning with writing five thankful and then slowly drifted toward the negative instead of focusing on the positive. Some days, you might need to start back over with your five thankfuls. Even if it's three in the afternoon!

Can you picture that moment on a roller coaster when you are slowly climbing up the hill and begin to level out at the top, there is this unexplainable anticipation before you fly down the slope. Life can be like that. At times, we feel like we are flying out of control.

The secret is knowing Who is in control when life doesn't feel stable. Although a rollercoaster feels beyond our control, the engineers who created it made sure to follow protocols and guidelines to ensure the safety of everyone who goes on it. Life with God feels like a spontanteous adventure. At times we wonder what God is up to and what tomorrow looks like. The future can be full of unknowns, but God is the Great Engineer and he is always working to create a path for you.

When we have days that feel shaky, unknown, or worrisome, we can do the following:

- Think about all the good things God has done in our lives.
- Invite Jesus into whatever is causing us that feeling of uncertainty.
- Repeat. Repeat. Repeat!

Yesterday, I had to do this four times! It was just one of those days. My circumstances didn't change, and everything was not immediately figured out, but after continually deciding to choose thankfulness and give God my stresses, I changed. And everyone in my house was glad of that! I ended the day on a positive note with laughter and fun.

Jesus, I am thankful for _____. I give You me (all my life stuff).Help me to remember throughout the day that I can give You everything and You will give me Your peace and laughter in exchange for my stresses. In Your name

Who can I give life to today?

What do I love?

1.
2.
3.
4.
5.

"This is how much God loved the world: He gave his Son, his one and only Son. And this is why: so that no one need be destroyed; by believing in him, anyone can have a whole and lasting life. God didn't go to all the trouble of sending his Son merely to point an accusing finger, telling the world how bad it was. He came to help, to put the world right again." (John 3:16-17 MSG)

The love of God is simple and complex! The simplicity is that we can choose to accept, believe, and embrace Jesus and give our lives to Him. These are simple steps that lead to Jesus living in us!

The complexity is remembering God's love in every moment. When life gets tough, we can forget that the same God who made the oceans and skies, and everything in between is also the God who takes care of us. We can forget that, in the end, everything is going to be perfect. We can forget that His love is big enough to cover all of our insecurity, pain, struggles and disappointment.

"For God so loved the world." That is you and me. He *so* loved us! Even when His love doesn't "feel" like enough to fill our heart, it is! Living life to the fullest is about embracing His love and choosing to shape our minds and lives around it.

God, when my thoughts go negative (about life, others, or myself) remind me that Your love is SO big. Help me to focus on the good things around me. In Jesus name

Who can I give life to today?

DAY 92

What am I thankful for?

1.
2.
3.
4.
5.

"You'll be your best by filling your minds and meditating on things TRUE..." (Phil. 4:8 MSG)

The continual battle of thinking great is real! We wake up in the morning and get to invite God into our day and think thankfulness. Then, we get in traffic or we are running late for school or work or somebody says or posts something mean... derailing our day. Maybe we started off the day thinking great but immediately because of life stuff, we go to a negative place. If we go to a negative place in our mind, we do not have to stay there.

No one can ruin our day. No circumstance can destroy our day. On even the worst of days, we can think of great things in our life and choose kindness to others. In the middle of a challenging day or hour, remembering the truth that God loves us and He is for us can change everything!

God, in the middle of situations, stop me from spiraling into negativity. Help me to think about Your truth continually. In Jesus name

Who can I give life to today?

What do I enjoy?

1.
2.
3.
4.
5.

"A joyful heart is good medicine..." *(Proverbs 17:22 ESV)*

Much of my life, my dad told me, "Life is a marathon, not a sprint, ENJOY the journey." What keeps us from enjoying the journey?

Worry can keep us from enjoying the journey. We worry about what others are thinking. We worry about whether we are good enough for the goal that we are striving to reach. We worry thinking, "do I have what it takes?" We worry about tomorrow.

Worry steals moments of JOY. Enjoying the journey consist of inviting God into our journey, fully living each moment, and being our very best in that moment.

We live in a society where we are all striving to reach the top, but are we having any fun on the journey? So many amazing talented people quit their dream, because stress consumes them. Exchanging JOY for worry is essential. If we choose to enjoy the journey instead of focusing on the destination- one day we will look around and realize that we are living a FULL life.

Do I enjoy each day or am I pushing myself so hard that my life is not fun?

God, help me to invite You into my thoughts, my words, my moments, my dreams, my journey. I choose Your joy instead of my worry. In Jesus name

Who can I give life to today?

DAY 94

What am I grateful for:

1.
2.
3.
4.
5.

"We demolish arguments and every pretension that sets itself up against the knowledge of God, and we take captive every thought to make it obedient to Christ." (2 Cor. 10:5 NIV)

"We demolish arguments!" Sometimes we have to argue with ourselves. Because of negative thinking habits or the enemy, we wrestle with defeating thoughts. Maybe we don't feel like we are enough, we wonder if we will ever get there, and we are aware of our failures. The negatives echo in our mind. We have a CHOICE to demolish all of this negativity that tries to argue with who we really are: "a masterpiece, a treasure, a conqueror, a chosen generation, sons and daughters of God..." We get to choose which thought to listen to. We don't have to let the negative beat us down. We can stop the self-defeating thoughts and focus on what God says about us.

What is one thing that God says about you than can be your "go to" thought when the negativity starts creeping in?

God, Help me to listen to what You call me, may Your voice drown out all the negativity, so I can live life to the FULLEST. In Jesus name

Who can I give life to today?

DAY 95

What is GREAT in my life?

1.
2.
3.
4.
5.

"You must have the same attitude that Christ Jesus had." *(Philippians 2:5 NIV)*

If I can't think of great things in my life..Maybe it is because I want to "get away" or escape?

If so, what do I want to get away from?

Maybe-the routine, responsibilities, the boring, and mundane... but that stuff is all there when I get back.

So maybe it's not getting away from it ALL…

What IF: it's just changing my attitude about all of my life stuff?

What if I chose to like who I am and the life I have?

What if I embrace my day with excitement, my routines with excellence, my boring with a smile, and my responsibilities with an attitude of laughter?

What if we approached every day every moment and gave it our best?

What would change if we are All IN -no matter what we're doing? What if we left every conversation, every task, every practice (sports or hobby), every day-grinning because we gave it our all?

If we give: Our best attitude, our greatest effort, while enjoying every moment, thinking great about others, about God, about ourselves=NO regret, for we can be "ALL IN." God, When I want a "day off from life" remind me of all the GREAT things in my life. Instead of hiding or running away- help me to JUMP-ALL IN. Help me to always look for the GOOD and may finding the good in life give me energy and joy. In Jesus name

Who can I give life to today?

DAY 96

What am I thankful for?

1.
2.
3.
4.
5.

"Since this is the kind of life we have chosen, the life of the Spirit...That means we will not compare ourselves with each other as if one of us were better and another worse. We have far more interesting things to do with our lives. Each of us is an original." (Galatians 5:25-26 MSG)

When we compare ourselves to others, it steals our joy. Sometimes we compare ourselves without even realizing it. We can usually find someone better and worse in every area. Competing in a world of achievers is hard. We have a tendency to wonder if we measure up. This verse says, *"We have far more interesting things to do with our lives. Each of us is an original."* God made us all originals, none of us are the exact same and none of us have the same God-given gifts, adventures, and dreams. So comparing ourselves is a waste of time.

What does the best version of me look like?

How do I become the best version of me?

What God-given gifts and talents do I have that will be life-giving to others?

How can I be the best version of me even when I am facing difficult challenges?

God, thank You for making me an original. Stop my thoughts when they want to go in a negative direction and compare myself to others. I invite You into every aspect of my life. In Jesus name

Who can I give life to today?

DAY 97

I am thankful for:

1.
2.
3.
4.
5.

"Go after a life of love as if your life depended on it—because it does."
(1 Corinthians 14:1 MSG)

There are a lot of verses about waiting and being still, but this one says, "GO!" It's talking about love. This verse has many dimensions. First, we must accept the love of God. He loves us to the core of our being. He loves us in our broken and messy, and in our great and thriving. The God of the Universe loves us with a love that knows no limits no boundaries. His love is big and sturdy enough to place our entire self-worth on. When we ask ourselves, "Do I measure up?" We can answer this question with, "I have worth because the God of the Universe made me and loves me." All the extras (titles, awards, achievements, compliments) are like icing on a cake, but a strong foundation to base our life on is found in the love of God.

How do we *"go after a life of love?"*

1. Everyday, when we wake up we can remind ourselves of God's great love for us.
2. When lies about our worth pop into our minds, we can stop and change those thoughts replacing them with what God says about us.

(Side note: There are so many verses in the Bible about what God says about us, "Masterpiece, treasure, royalty, His sons and daughters.)

3. We can constantly give His love to others.

We can always choose to go after a life of love!

God, show me what it means to base my worth in Your love, and to go after a life of love. I invite Jesus to change my negative thoughts about me. Show me who to reach out to today.

Who can I give life to today?

DAY 98

I woke up thankful for:

1.
2.
3.
4.
5.

"I'm bankrupt without love, love never gives up." (1 Corinthians 13:7 MSG)

The Source of love (God) never gives up. He pursues us, forgives us, gives us hope, and promises peace. His love for us is like a never ending river flowing from His heart to ours. It's where that inner thirst is quenched. Nothing else fills us, our hearts were made to be continually filled with His love.

It's easy to try to fill up our schedules with fun things. We can hope that movies, video games, social media and other people will either give us hope, or numb us to what's really going on. All these things are fun, yet all of these leave us unsatisfied and wanting more.

How am I doing today? Am I thirsty for something?

God's love is constantly pursuing us. His love can drive out hopelessness and sadness. Living in Him is key in every season.

We can wake up and spend a few minutes with God, remind ourselves throughout the day that He is with us and for us, and whisper a prayer of thanks before we go to sleep. We can live full when we choose to live aware of God throughout the day. We can live full of His love, regardless of our circumstances.

God, I choose to live in Your love. Saturate my heart with Your love and hope. Remind me that Your love is the Source of life. I give You me. In Jesus name

Who can I give life to today?

DAY 99

What am I thankful for?

1.
2.
3.
4.
5.

"Trust in the Lord with all your heart and lean not on your own understanding; in all your ways submit to him, and he will make your paths straight." (Proverbs 3:5-6 NIV)

Personalizing Scripture helps us grow in our walk with God. One way to do this is to read a verse and ask ourselves questions about it. For instance, in this verse we can ask:

- Do I trust that God is for me and loves me?
- What part of my heart am I not trusting God with (my future, this situation, a relationship)?
- What do I fear could happen?

- Will I invite God into my situation by praying and submitting it to Him?
- Will I follow His way for me?

When we break apart a verse by asking ourselves questions, we face our thoughts and we can be real with God. God loves us completely. He also already knows us inside and out, so our answers don't surprise Him. We get to choose to trust Him, to let go of our own way of dealing with things, to submit to Him, and ask Him to show us the way.

God, help me to trust you no matter what. Even when I am facing something new or unknown, help me to trust that Your heart for me is good, which leads me to give You control. Show me Your way for me. In Jesus name

Who can I give life to today?

DAY 100

What makes me smile?

1.
2.
3.
4.
5.

"I've found the recipe for being happy whether full or hungry, hands full or hands empty. Whatever I have, wherever I am, I can make it through anything in the One who makes me who I am." (Philippians 4:12-13 MSG)

Life isn't easy. We go through ups and downs emotionally, in relationships, at school, at work, and in our dreams and goals.

Do I believe God is always with me?

Can I continue growing in my relationship with Him? How?

How have my thoughts changed and my faith grown over the last 100 days?

"I can make it through ANYTHING in the ONE who makes me who I am." I love this translation. God is the one who makes us who we are. We can find our worth in Him. His heart is love, so to Him we are all lovable. This truth gives me great peace when it feels like life is tough.

In my thoughts, do I constantly remember that I am lovable and have great worth simply because He made me and He loves me?

God, remind me often who I am in You. In Jesus name

Who can I give life to today?

KEEP GOING!

"I (Jesus) have come that they may have life, and have it to the full!"
(John 10:10 NIV)

Jesus has a full life for everyone, it may not mean a perfect life, but our heart can be full because we are growing in our relationship with God who loves us and is FOR us.

Spending time with God is simple:

1. Start off thankful and jumpstart your brain by asking yourself, what are five good things in my life? What am I thankful for?
2. Read a Bible verse and ask yourself questions about how this verse applies to you personally,
3. Invite Jesus into every aspect of life (thoughts, relationships, moments, dreams, school/work, struggles).

Repeatedly doing these three things changes our perspective. When we *think* thankful, we *feel* thankful and we live this out by the way we treat others. Doing this affects everything in our life. When we grow in our faith, our life becomes better!

*If you enjoyed this book, check out *Choose Life to the Fullest* Books 1-3-! Written in the same format; days 91-100 were from these books.

AUTHOR'S NOTE FROM MICAH

"As an Arizona Diamondback, I saw Micah consistently put his faith in action on a daily basis, in times of trial and in triumph. It was obvious to me, and to those around him, that his walk with God was solid. To understand the incredible value and absolute necessity of creating and maintaining a daily spiritual routine is vital to every believer, young and old. In this devotional, Becca and Micah have prepared a beautiful introduction and outline to inspire and challenge each of us to consistently and intentionally walk with God daily, which can and will grow our faith in every circumstance. I have sincerely loved reading this devotional each day."

Dan Carlson, Arizona Diamondbacks Minor
League Pitching Coordinator

First of all, I want to THANK YOU if you are reading this! I also want to thank my dear sister, Becca, for inviting me to write the 4ᵗʰ *Choose* book with her. Thank You, Jesus!

Whether you were gifted our book or purchased…thank you! All the credit goes to my Father up above and the journey He has blessed me on.

Speaking of this journey, it has not always been pleasant and there have been many challenges, heartaches, blood, sweat, and tears. Much of my most challenging times is when I have turned to writing. Some of the devotions were pulled from the past twenty years of journaling throughout my career (amateur and professional) and life. However, a large portion of my writing in these pages has come from the past year.

While I've experienced A LOT throughout my career, the past year has been one of the most challenging ever. Many of you will agree. The pandemic and Covid19 have brought challenges that none of us could have ever imagined. Perhaps the toughest thing ever, many of us were forced to 'social distance' from those closest to us. We could not embrace our loved ones with a hug and kiss. Even worse, we were told to stay within six feet from each other and wear a mask. My family and I personally experienced my Father going through heart surgery in the month of June 2020. The procedure and recovery ended up being much more severe than the doctors anticipated. Thankfully, God was in my Father and the doctor's midst with a successful surgery. Much of what you will read, I wrote during this time.

During this same time in June, I went through a heartbreaking separation with someone whom I love dearly. Much of what you will read, I wrote during this time. I share all this because it is important for you to know that as I wrote, I didn't have it all together. In fact, many of the devotions I was digging down and searching deep By the way, what does having it all together even mean? For me, having faith, that God is with you always and that He never leaves you is a good first step. Experiencing a real, authentic relationship with our Father is truly amazing.

Acknowledging that Jesus defeated death and rose for me to experience this relationship with Him brings me such humility and appreciation. For I died and rose with Jesus because of Jesus! As I journal almost every day, I thank my Father (for life, for being with me, and for being my Father)! I also welcome the Holy Spirit to open my eyes and ears to what God is trying to teach me. For He is always speaking to us and teaching us. As you read, know that God is with you and loves you so very much! At times, we don't feel his love nor do we think we deserve it, but

He is WITH you and LOVES you! All you have to do is seek Him! He is continually waiting to spend time with you and can't wait for you to come to Him (no matter how good or bad you think you are or things are). May these devotionals from my dear sister and I speak to you and help you experience our Father's love deeper than ever before! Some of my favorite verses: Philippians 4:13, Micah 6:8, Jeremiah 29:11, Proverbs 3:5-6, Psalm 46:10, Proverbs 27:17…

Blessings and Love-MO

Story of this Series

Thinking thankful repeatedly transforms negative thinking, daily inviting Jesus in is life-changing. After almost 20 years of counseling adolescents, I realized that I needed a curriculum that could completely change the thought process. I desperately wanted this for each of the teens that came to me for counseling or mentoring, I kept looking for a short, daily, six month curriculum that would provide this.

When my own 16-year-old son spiraled into negativity and self-destructive thinking, I started writing daily thought devotions @chooselifetothefullest and paid him to edit. I believed this routine could save him from self-destruction and depression. My heart's greatest desire for him was transformation of his thought process and developing his faith.

The routine is simple: writing five things he was thankful for every morning, reading a verse while asking himself questions about his own personal faith, and closing with the short prayer to invite Jesus into everything!

Publishing was not part of the plan until one of his friends asked me to publish, and 90 days of devotions was the plan not 360, but my son kept reading and so I kept writing. When he turned 18, I realized I had just watched a miracle unfold before my eyes, I get teary-eyed every time that I share our story. "Mom, I'm not sure when, but at some point I started liking myself and realizing God is for me and has a plan for me." My son thinks healthy, which has improved his performance in every area of his life, and most importantly he has a growing relationship with Jesus Christ.

You see, waking up and choosing to think thankful, eventually leads to thinking thankful throughout the day, and spending time with Jesus is transforming, furthermore inviting Jesus into everything leads to life to the fullest. (John 10:10)

Choose life to the Fullest –90 Days to thinking and living great –books 1, 2, and 3 all have the same format and can be read in any order, for they are not sequential. *Choose Life to the Fullest* book 4 is co-authored with my brother, Micah Owings, who I loved watching live out his dreams on the field. This book is written specifically for dreamers, go-getters, and athletes.

Because I believe in this practice, everyday I wake up and write my thankfuls, my husband Dan and my five kids (Owin, Addi, Eben, JohnE, Anden) are always on this list. Our home is full of blessed chaos and laughter, spills and messes, sports of all sorts and Addi's art, friends and family, realness and prayers. Love living moments to the fullest!

- Becca

REFERENCES

Batterson, M. (2016) *Chase the lion*. The Crown Publishing Group.

Disney, W (n. d.) *First, think. Second, believe. Third, dream. And finally, dare.*

, J. (2020). *Get your life back: Everyday practices for a world gone mad*. Thomas Nelson.

Manning, B. (2009) *The Furious longings of God*

Newberry, T. (2012). *40 days to a joy-filled life*. Tyndale House Publishers.

Rohn, J. (n. d.) *You can't change your destination overnight…*

Sinach (2015). *Way maker*. Nigeria, Africa: Loveworld SLIC

Smykowski, J. (2021, Feb 5). *What is the real definition of a true friend?* betterhelp.com